Transport and Industrial Heritage
Cornwall

Above: Lime kilns were used for producing lime to neutralise acidic soils but surviving examples on the North Cornish coast are few and far between. This excellent specimen is at Boscastle, SX 098913, seen in 2008, after the great flood. *Author*

Below: This old abandoned slate quarry in the Trebarwith Valley at SX 072863 is overlooked by the impressive Prince of Wales Quarry engine house of about 1870 vintage. A trail passes through the part-overgrown and flooded waste dumps. *Author*

Transport and Industrial Heritage

Cornwall

John Vaughan

Ian Allan
PUBLISHING

First published 2009

ISBN 978 0 7110 3372 6

Published by Ian Allan Publishing

an imprint of Ian Allan Publishing Ltd, Hersham, Surrey KT12 4RG
Printed in England by Ian Allan Printing Ltd, Hersham, Surrey KT12 4RG

Code: 0905/B2

Visit the Ian Allan Publishing website at
www.ianallanpublishing.com

Acknowledgements

As with any project of this size and breadth it has been necessary to call upon a number of research institutions and individuals for illustrations and specialist information. I must say that I was greatly impressed by the cheerful co-operation received and the natural enthusiasm shown by all contributors who were positive not only about their particular sphere of interest but by the project generally.

In no particular order I would like to sincerely thank Kim Cooper and her willing staff at the Cornish Studies Library in Redruth; John Aanonson of Brunel University at Runnymede; Joyce Greenham of the Newquay Old Cornwall Society, Newquay Library; the Cornwall County Records Office at Truro; Robert Cook of the Royal Institution of Cornwall at Truro; Penzance Corporation; Peter Waller and the Ian Allan Library; Maurice Dart; Peter Treloar; Alan Lambert; Bill Walker; John Hicks; and all contributing photographers, who are duly credited at the end of each caption. I would also like to thank the authors of a vast number of specialist publications dealing with a diverse range of subjects. Other reference documents and publications consulted include various railway magazines, old Cornish newspapers and manuscripts and literally hundreds of books, too many to include in a detailed bibliography.

Contents

Note: All 'SX', 'SS' and 'SW' approximate map references refer to the 1:50,000 Ordnance Survey maps

Introduction

Cornwall is a special place. Hundreds if not thousands of books have been written about the county describing some particular aspect of its history or topography, many of them in glowing and romantic terms. Every corner has been explored and written about, from the high moorlands to the rugged cliff scenery and small fishing villages dotted along the breathtaking coastline. Cornwall's Celtic origins and folklore seem to fascinate, and whether it be inhabitants from the Iron Age, the Romans, the Saxons or those in the far south-west in medieval times, the history of the county is unique. The Cornish language survives, albeit not in everyday conversation, and it has strong links with the ancient languages of Wales, Scotland, Ireland and north-west France.

Many of Cornwall's ancient stone monuments are thousands of years old and most promote some form of superstition. Churches, ancient castles and the legend of King Arthur all keep a combination of myths and truths alive. Tales of smuggling and the earliest days of sail seem to fascinate. Cornwall's fauna, flora and wildlife are of interest mainly because the climate lends itself to seasonal growth and activity that is not shared by the rest of the UK. Bird life in particular is found in abundance. Above all else, and in the eyes of many commentators, Cornwall is almost an island, 'separated' from Devon and the rest of the UK by the famous River Tamar.

In late-Victorian times, once the railway and other modern forms of transport had become firmly established, the tourist industry was born, which has led to an annual invasion of the county's many attractions. Until perhaps 30 to 40 years ago Cornwall managed to preserve a unique atmosphere akin to going back in time, but since then there has been a massive influx of British immigrants looking for a better quality of life and perhaps a different pace of life. In certain parts of Cornwall this has been self-defeating as the population is now well in excess of half a million and there are some fairly hideous traffic jams around St Austell and Truro, especially during peak periods. There seem to be few born-and-bred Cornishmen in the pubs and the

The minerals primarily mined in Cornwall were copper, tin and, to a lesser extent, lead, iron, zinc, wolfram and arsenic. Adjacent to the St Ives to St Just road on the north coast are two ruined engine houses that were once part of the Carn Galver Mine (SW 421364). These fine examples, showing the pumping engine nearest the camera and the whim engine beyond, had 40-inch and 20-inch steam engines fitted. Decay has been arrested by the efforts of the National Trust. *Author*

The County of Cornwall is littered with hundreds of abandoned engine houses – indeed they have become synonymous with the great 19th-century mining era, which formed an important part of the Cornish industrial revolution. The abandoned buildings come in various shapes and sizes and some are situated at breathtaking locations. This view shows the Wheal Trewavas houses (SW 600265) between Marazion and Helston on the south coast. This old copper mine was worked under the sea and was eventually closed by flooding. *Author*

The mighty River Tamar is the border between Cornwall and Devon and the first railway station on the Cornish side of the river is Saltash. Cornwall County Council and the First Great Western train operator have erected bilingual welcoming signs on the platforms featuring the Royal Albert Bridge. The Cornish language survives but sees little everyday use. *Author*

Cornish culture has been diluted. However, what cannot be taken from Cornwall is its great industrial past and its transport history, with remains surviving in their thousands and all, in various ways, worth visiting and exploring.

There is no doubt that if a single edifice had to be selected as an icon to represent Cornwall, it would undoubtedly be an old abandoned engine house from the mid-Victorian era, standing silently as a left-over from the heyday of Cornish mining, about 150 years ago. Centuries ago tin mining by streaming in the Cornish rivers had taken place. Indeed, it was one of the reasons why there was an active trade with Mediterranean countries in Roman times, some 2,000 years ago. However, the entire scale of operations changed in the late 18th century when mining started to scratch below the surface in the search for richer lodes of tin, copper and lead. There was also some iron-mining activity, but not on the same scale as other minerals. The deeper the mines went, the greater the water ingress and the greater the need for machinery to haul men and ore to the surface and to pump water out of the mine.

Once there was an established requirement for machinery it needed to be powered, which was provided by manpower, horsepower, water power and eventually steam power. Once water-wheels became part of the power solution, water had to be channelled away from rivers and streams, in some cases for several miles in artificial leats. However, that source was not always reliable and the power output was limited. This shortcoming required the engineers and inventors to find mechanical ways to perform a wide range of tasks, leading to some incredible ingenuity at the beginning of the 19th

The County of Cornwall is riddled with industrial and transport architecture from a bygone age. In this view, now totally obscured by foliage, the old single track to Moorswater disappears under the narrow road bridge at Coombe Junction, adjacent to the old Looe Union Canal.

Class 37 No 37675 *William Cookworthy* (the discoverer of china clay in Cornwall) rides high on Moorswater Viaduct with down china clay wagons on 4 April 1990. The remains of the clay hood wagon was a left-over from a past runaway. *Author*

Above: Cornwall is an ancient land with Celtic origins dating back to about 350BC. Roaming tribes located there when they discovered tin in abundance. For centuries Cornish inhabitants retained their independence and, indeed, in the 13th-century Mappa Mundi the four parts of the 'Island of Britain' are shown as England, Scotland, Wales and Cornwall! There are ancient monuments in many locations, such as the Hurlers at Minions, Hut Circles near Dozemary Pool, and King Doniat's stone near St Cleer. These delightful headstones can be found in St Winnow's churchyard on the banks of the River Fowey at SX 115570. *Author*

century from the likes of Cornishman Richard Trevithick. Early crude steam engines became more sophisticated and later much larger and more efficient. When stationary steam engines started to grow in size and number, the amount of coal required to fire them grew, and as Cornwall had no coalfields or mines this all had to be imported. Similarly, as the output from the mines increased, so the need for a reliable form of transport, with a greater capacity compared to the pack animals that had been used for centuries, became necessary.

This requirement resulted in the first horse-drawn wagons appearing, followed by horse tramways and finally railways. The inter-relationship between industry and transport again came to the fore when an urgent requirement to improve Cornwall's roads emerged and Turnpike Trusts were created. The roads were improved, but at a cost that could only be recovered through tolls. Once improved, the roads were used by a new form of transport; stagecoaches and mail coaches. This in turn promoted the mobility of the general public, at least the middle and upper classes, and coaches were soon connecting with ships, particularly from Hayle to Bristol, where eventually passengers could catch a train to London. Also, throughout Cornwall, but particularly across the south coast estuaries, there were a large number of ferries ranging from rowing boats to small ships. Some of these river and channel crossings can be traced back several hundred years, although the busiest crossing at Torpoint dates back only to the early 19th century. These ferries are still very much a part of the Cornish transport infrastructure of the 21st century and they save every traveller several miles compared with land-borne alternatives.

The greater the output from the mines, the greater the requirement for ships. At the start of the 18th century and for the next 100 years most vessels were small wooden sailing ships ranging from 30 to about 250 tons. These ships had to be small in order to enter Cornwall's many restricted tidal harbours or to simply 'beach' in the sandy bays. Mining was not seasonal and during the winter months these small ships continued working, plying from Cornwall to various parts of the UK and nearer Europe. They were very vulnerable in storms and heavy seas. So many were wrecked and so many lives were lost that lighthouses, the Coastguard and the Lifeboat institutions were established. An early solution to inland transport problems elsewhere in the UK was shipment by canal, but the Cornish terrain did not really lend itself to this mode of transport and only about half a dozen examples were ever built. Nevertheless, some operated successfully for several decades.

As soon as the Industrial Revolution hit Cornwall there was a requirement for many support industries, for example foundries, engineering works, smelters, brickworks, explosives factories and the like. However, an industry that will always be associated with

Railway Terrace, Carharrack

Above: Once the Industrial Revolution got under way and the various types of mining became established on a significant scale, the labour-intensive activities needed populating and a whole range of facilities were required for the thousands of manual workers, including housing. This typical terrace of granite dwellings is located at Carharrack in the heart of the St Day mining district. In the foreground of this Edwardian scene is the Redruth & Chasewater Railway, which opened in 1824 and closed in 1915. *Cornish Studies Library*

PLACE '' AND CHURCH, FOWEY   11052

In the early days of the industrial revolution a number of important and powerful Cornish families came to the fore, based primarily on their extensive mine and land holdings. One of the most dynamic families was the Treffrys, whose 'seat' was at 'Place' in the town of Fowey. The family owned the local docks, mines, pits and vast tracts of agricultural land. Joseph Thomas Treffry was a key figure in the development of ports, canals and tramways. In this delightful scene from the 1920s, 'Place', Fowey Church and a Western National bus for St Blazey and Par are featured. *Author's collection*

Cornwall is china clay and china stone extraction. By the mid-1860s the Cornish metalliferous mining industry was in steep decline and, although the china clay industry started in a rather small way, to some extent it filled an enormous vacuum in terms of employment; it was to become colossal and was Cornwall's main employer in manpower terms. Millions of tons would be produced every year for an immense range of applications. In the 21st century it remains an important Cornish industry and although there have been recent manpower reductions it is still a major employer.

The first long-distance horse-worked tramway was opened in 1812, followed shortly by two more lines, built to connect the mines and the pits with ports. Again technology took a hand when steam locomotives began to appear in Cornwall from 1834, the first being on the standard gauge Bodmin & Wadebridge Railway. This was followed in 1837 by the Hayle Railway, which was absorbed by the West Cornwall Railway in 1852. However, in the eyes of many it was the opening of the Cornwall Railway's broad gauge main line from Plymouth and across the River Tamar to Truro in 1859 and Falmouth in 1863 that opened the transport door by linking Cornwall with the rest of the UK by rail. Eventually a comprehensive railway network would develop, which would include main lines, branch lines and mineral lines with various operators. From 1892 all of these lines, except minor mineral tramways, conformed to standard gauge.

There were many other extractive industries, one of the main ones being quarrying. Although this was mainly for granite, which could be found in abundance in Cornwall, it also included high-quality slate and even roadstone. Cornwall had a wide range of industries, some of which dated back centuries, such as burning limestone in lime kilns and importing sand from the seashore for agricultural purposes and farming generally. Other activities included textile mills, flower-growing, brewing and, above all else, fishing. In a county surrounded by water, with long north and south coasts, it was natural that part of the staple diet would come from the sea. At one time almost every town, village and hamlet on the coast would have a fishing industry. Despite government and European interference with fishing quotas and other draconian policies, there is still a buoyant fishing business, at Newlyn in particular.

Being at the south-western extremity of the UK it was natural that, once modern communications via submarine cables and wireless transmissions started, Cornwall's geographical position would put the county in the forefront. It was as early as 1870 at Porthcurno that the first cable was laid. Eventually it would be the centre for 14 cables to many different parts of the world; there is a museum at SW 384227. In addition to cables, Cornwall was involved in the early days of radio transmission when Marconi was active in the Lizard area, using a cliff top at Poldhu to transmit the first transatlantic signal in 1901. The site became a wireless telegraphy station and lasted until 1933; there is a monument at SW 664194.

Towards the end of the 19th and the beginning of the 20th century, technology was changing and both electricity and the internal combustion engine were being developed as quickly as the steam engine had been a century earlier. This had an impact on both industry and transport. As early as 1902 a street tramway system was up and running between Redruth and Camborne, steam traction engines were performing a range of tasks, and by 1903 the Great Western Railway (GWR) was running a number of motor bus services. These services were closely followed by motor lorries, providing the start of a goods-by-road transport explosion.

The motor car started to appear in Cornwall at the turn of the 20th century and, in common with every other part of the UK, automobiles would have a greater impact on society over the next century than anything that had gone before. By the 21st century there were more than 320,000 cars and vans registered in the county! Major new road schemes were undertaken, subject to the Cornwall County Council highways budget.

As early as 1910 the first Cornish flight had taken place when a primitive Farman biplane had flown over the fleet anchored in Mount's Bay. This was the start of a new mode of transport in Cornwall, which is now rapidly approaching its centenary. Both airships and fixed-wing aircraft were based in Cornwall during the First and Second World Wars when the county really came into its own with many bases at a variety of locations. The first passenger-carrying commercial flights started in the 1930s and, except for the war years, business has been growing. In particular the number of passengers transported between Penzance Heliport and Land's End and Newquay airports on the Cornish mainland and the Isles of Scilly has grown to nearly 300,000 per annum. Newquay Airport started life as part of the military RAF St Mawgan but is now independent and the Cornish town is now accessible from all over the UK with 400,000 users annually.

LANDING FISH. ST IVES.

Although mining has always been important in Cornwall, fishing greatly pre-dates mineral extraction. Ports of various size are located all around Cornwall's famous coastline and historically all have been involved in fishing activities. Over the years Government and European legislation has had a negative impact on the industry in terms of catch quotas. With one or two exceptions recreational sailing activities have replaced fishing at many locations. In this wonderful old tinted postcard, fish are being loaded into carts in the harbour at St Ives. *Author's collection*

Over the past three centuries the most remarkable phenomenon has been the development of the tourist industry. It has been stated that, once the Falmouth railway branch line opened in 1863, tourists started to arrive and shortly afterwards the first purpose-built hotel was built. There had of course always been inns for people to stay in, but the scale of the accommodation required for tourists was in another league. Newquay was one of the fastest-growing towns where the growth could be attributable almost entirely to tourism. By the late Victorian era vast hotels were being built adjacent to the Towan Headland area, followed by numerous modest establishments. In these early days, before the advent of the motor car or the aeroplane, the railways had a major influence in promoting holiday traffic through advertising and offers. Before long there were through trains from London and other major cities to the prime resorts. The heyday for the railways was in the late 1930s and the mid-1950s, but changing annual leave patterns, the remarkable growth in the ownership of motor cars by the new affluent society and the arrival of the package holiday and cheap flights had a severe impact on the number of holidaymakers arriving by train. Overall business has recovered and not only has the Cornish population grown far beyond the half million mark but the latest figures show that 5¼ million people visit Cornwall every year. The season is getting longer and several new sources of traffic have emerged, such as surfers and water sport fans. Also individual attractions, such as the Eden Centre, have pulled in the crowds. A glimpse at one of the racks of brochures for tourists at prime Cornish locations shows many hundreds of sites offering some form of entertainment for visitors.

It would be easy to be negative about the state of industry in Cornwall, especially when one views the derelict engine houses and mining remains from times past. Other than for the wealthy mine-owning and land-owning families, Cornwall has, historically, not been a prosperous county and unemployment levels have traditionally been higher in the Royal Duchy than elsewhere in the UK. The great days of mining have gone forever, although every time prices on the world commodities market increase there is a re-examination of the viability of Cornish mines. The china clay industry is now in French ownership and its fortunes have been mixed; however, at the time of writing the industry remains important to Cornwall's economy. Whatever the state of the economy the population is increasing; until recently house prices were booming and in the last couple of decades tens of thousands of people have decided that Cornwall is where they want to live.

In this book I have attempted to give a broad overview of the history and subsequent developments of past and present industry and transportation in Cornwall. Some of the industries ceased operations over a century ago while others have survived the passage of time and continue into the 21st century. Inevitably with such a wide range of topics it has been necessary to apply a very 'broad brush' approach in describing, in a few paragraphs, a subject that could easily fill a massive tome. However, the objective has been fourfold: to provide a wide-ranging background to each subject; to provide interesting past and present illustrations; to give the locations of a sample of sites worth visiting; and to give the reader an incentive for further self-study. This volume could not possibly have been undertaken without the valuable help of a large number of individuals and institutions, and in the Acknowledgements I express my sincere gratitude to all contributors. I sincerely hope that this book will give the reader the same amount of enjoyment as I have experienced in its execution. Happily its publication coincides with the 200th anniversary of the Poldice Tramway, the 175th anniversary of the Bodmin & Wadebridge Railway, the 150th anniversary of the Royal Albert Bridge and the Cornwall Railway and (almost) the 100th anniversary of the first flight in Cornwall.

Finally, I would like to dedicate this book to my old and loyal friend Peter Garnett of Worthing, who has been a positive and encouraging influence in all that I have done for more than five decades. Thank you, Peter.

John Vaughan
Goring by Sea,
March 2009

A roadside relic at Angarrack seen in 2002. Gwinear Road station closed in 1964! *Author*

THE RAILWAYS AND
BRANCHES OF CORNWALL

Legend:
-------- = Narrow Gauge

Mining

In industrial terms one of the primary associations with Cornwall is mining. If individual counties had symbols applied to car registration plates, as seen throughout the USA, there is little doubt that those in Cornwall would carry the image of an abandoned engine house, depicting one of the hundreds of long-closed mines.

The history of mining in Cornwall can be traced back thousands of years to prehistoric times. By the Middle Ages the importance of mining had grown considerably and many activities were administered centrally, through such institutions as stannary courts. In these early days, especially with tin mining, much of the activity was at surface level and involved 'streaming', where the valley gravels in rivers and streams were the primary source. It was the same in the early days of mining throughout the world; for example, the image of old gold miners in the 1840s panning for gold in a river and finding a nugget, or at least a good sprinkling of gold dust, was the stuff of which movies were made. These gravels were washed by miners to remove the lighter materials in order to gradually refine the tin-bearing residues.

Once extracted, the tin had to be smelted and purified and some ancient Cornish ingots from Roman times have been found. At this time tin was used in everything from church bells to armaments. As early as 1201 there were charters giving prospectors,

Life for underground miners was a miserable existence, as exemplified in this remarkable photograph from 1892, taken at East Pool mine. In hot, dark and damp conditions, with only a handful of candles for illumination (located on the front of their headgear), these miners have a short break to eat their pasties or to have a puff on their clay pipes. With the visibly low headroom and dressed in their inevitably grubby clothes, nobody is smiling for the photographer! Note the underground tramway, used for conveying mined ores. *Cornish Studies Library*

The heyday of the Cornish mining industry was in the 1850s and 1860s. Over the years there was extreme volatility in the international commodities market, and the prices obtained for extracted minerals were subject to regular crashes. Such periods resulted in considerable unemployment in Cornwall and many Cornishmen emigrated to all parts of the world, especially Australia and the USA, where their experience was invaluable. Some mines struggled on into the 20th century and this view shows Goonvean mine in July 1955. Note the pile of coal, necessary to feed the boilers to power the vast beam engine. *Author's collection*

or tinners as they were to become known, many rights including permissions to search for and dig for tin on unenclosed common land.

Some early tin mines are known to have been working in Cornwall in the 15th century, and gradually over time such workings became larger and more numerous. The main mining area was around Camborne and Redruth, but there were significant workings north of Liskeard, above the River Tamar west of Gunnislake, on the north coast between St Just and St Agnes and in the greater Helston area. As distinct from copper, tin was always smelted within Cornwall and the furnaces at these locations produced 'white tin'. In the 19th century there were several periods when world commodity prices were extremely low and the Cornish tin-mining industry gradually dwindled. Nevertheless tin smelting did not finally end until the Cornish Smelting Company's works near Redruth closed during 1931.

The problem was that these relatively easy pickings soon ran out and greater effort had to made to find most precious metals. Basically this meant moving earth, rocks, hills and mountains, or, as in the majority of cases, digging downward in an attempt to find a lode of

Tramways in mines greatly pre-date normal surface railway lines in Cornwall. Many mines had extensive tramways both above and below ground and, by way of example, in 1783 it was reported that the Happy Union mine near Pentewan had a complete underground system. On some of these lines trucks were simply pushed by hand, some were cable-hauled, and horses and ponies were also employed. In this spectacular picture a battery locomotive is seen in Cook's shaft at South Crofty near Illogan on 6 January 1953. *Cornish Studies Library, courtesy of M. Dart*

the appropriate rock or ore. Initially this was done by pick and shovel, but from the late 18th and early 19th centuries life was made easier, or at least less labour-intensive, by the use of machinery. This machinery became ever more sophisticated and larger in scale over time. Important engineers and inventors were forever seeking better ways of extracting the raw material, increasing volumes, and processing and transporting the product.

In the early days a combination of manual labour and animal power turned machinery and hauled loads, but the main energy source was from water-wheels. These water-wheels and associated machinery were placed at convenient locations beside rivers and streams, but where mines were away from any natural water source the water was diverted and carried in flumes or leats to the remote water-wheel. By the late 18th and 19th centuries steam power became all-important, not only in terms of mine excavation but also in lifting minerals from the ground, pumping vast volumes of water from the mines, which in many areas was an ever-present hazard with a high flooding risk, and for conveying workers to the various underground levels in the mines.

Above: An example of a horse-powered tramway system is seen here at Robinson's shaft, South Crofty, near Illogan. Five small tippler wagons loaded with crushed ore are about to leave the site. In the background is the remarkable stamping house, where mined ore was crushed for transportation to a smelter. Note the vast superstructure and the inevitable stack behind. *Cornish Studies Library, courtesy of M. Dart*

Although mining for tin was one of the earliest recorded activities, in terms of sheer volume copper mining was to become hugely more important in Cornwall. Copper mining on any scale worth mentioning started in the 16th century and over the next 300 years the industry was to grow to become one of the major employers in the county. One of the problems with copper mining was that many tons of ore had to be mined in order to extract a single ton of copper. This extraction through the smelting process requires heat provided by furnaces and in this era the primary fuel was coal. So much coal was used that it made economic sense to locate the smelters near the coal mines. With a handful of exceptions in the Hayle area this meant transporting large volumes of heavy ore over poor roads and using small-capacity sailing ships to reach the main smelters in South Wales.

Some of the output figures were, even by today's standards, impressive. For example, nearly 1 million tons were produced in the Gwennap and St Day areas between 1815 and 1872. The largest of the mines produced hundreds of thousands of tons of ore, but the more that was extracted the deeper the mines became. The deepest mine in Cornwall was Dalcoath, where workings extended to 3,300 feet beneath the ground. This required mining in more difficult circumstances and water removal rates needed to increase, resulting in larger and larger steam pumping engines, which consumed more and more coal. There came a point where the cost of extraction exceeded the price that could be achieved for the ore, especially in any periods of downturn.

In the middle of the 19th century Cornwall became the biggest copper producer in the world, until it was overtaken by certain South American countries. Substantial new sources were subsequently found in Australia and in North and South America and this had a lasting impact on prices. Peak output in Cornwall occurred in 1856. In the mid-1860s there was a slump of catastrophic proportions and Cornish mines closed in large numbers. The resulting unemployment caused severe social problems and significant numbers of Cornish miners emigrated to find employment in the very places where new mineral discoveries had been made.

The industry struggled on, but further discoveries in Malaya and, at the turn of century, in Bolivia resulted in further large-scale closures in the 1890s and a virtual end

Mines and mine buildings came in every shape and size. These derelict and silent monuments once housed large steam engines that were used to pump water from the mines. Water ingress was phenomenal and the wetter the mine, the larger the pumping engine needed to be. Steam engines were also used as winding engines, often abbreviated to 'whims', for raising ore and materials but also to drive stamps or ore-crushers. These relics are near Trewavas Head on Cornwall's south coast. *Author*

to the industry in Cornwall by the year 1900. There were a couple of periods when there was a minor revival in fortunes but the halcyon days had gone forever. Although a couple of mines struggled on until the end of the 20th century and a speculative restart at South Crofty mine was considered in 2007, the Cornish copper-mining industry has effectively passed into history.

In addition to tin and copper a number of other minerals were mined throughout Cornwall. One of the more important metals was lead, which was mined in some volume. The most important areas were near Liskeard and at East Wheal Rose mine, near Newlyn East, which produced more than half of Cornwall's total lead output of 21,000 tons in 1845. From 1849 it was served by an early horse-worked tramway linking it with the nearby harbour at Newquay. Lead was also smelted within Cornwall, and Joseph Thomas Treffry built a vast lead smelter at Par, which had a 600yd-long flue and a colossal 248-foot-high chimney (see page 33). Again the output was ingots of lead that were exported by ship, mainly to London. Silver could be found in some of the lead ores and this was extracted and sold almost as a by-product of lead extraction.

Another important mineral was iron ore, although sadly commercial exploitation was also overtaken by falling world commodity prices. There were early mines in the Restormel area and elsewhere, but it was the Perran Iron Lode south of Newquay and near the holiday beach at Holywell Bay that had the most potential. The Cornish Consolidated Iron Mines Company was formed to extract iron ore from the Perran Lode and at one time there were no fewer than 25 mines open in the Gravel Hill area. However, by 1874 this had reduced to just seven and by 1880 or thereabouts iron mining in the area had finished, another victim of falling prices.

Zinc was produced in Cornwall as a by-product of copper, tin and lead mining and processing. It was used in galvanising processes, in the manufacture of brass, and for sheeting with low corrosive qualities. Wolfram, used in tungsten light filaments, was also produced as a by-product of tin mining. Another substance emanating from Cornwall, particularly in the 19th century, was arsenic, an impurity found in tin ores, which was extracted by calcining. The fumes given off by the process were poisonous and taller stacks were provided for such works to disperse the gases more widely! The diverse uses for arsenic include insecticides for use in agriculture, wood treatment and pharmaceuticals.

If one had to select a period when Cornish mining, in all its guises, was at its peak it would be the mid-19th century. The remarkable levels of activity made Cornwall a world leader in terms of output, with the renowned skill of the workforce being spread throughout the world by circumstance. What also becomes apparent as the subject is further explored is that mining, machinery, power generation and the various modes of transport are inextricably linked and each will be generally described throughout this book.

Basset Mines

The highly recommended Great Flat Lode heritage trail, which includes the Basset Mines complex (SX 681394), is well signposted. The Bassets were one of the most famous, wealthy and influential families in Cornwall. Their name was incorporated in the names of many old mines, public buildings, street names and even a cove near

The Basset Mines form part of the Great Flat Lode to the south of Carn Brea, a significant local landmark on the south side of a line between Redruth and Camborne. The landscape is unique and, after the publication of a 1989 survey report by the Cornwall Archaeological Unit into the Central Mining District of Cornwall, it became a proposed World Heritage Site. A number of routes were proposed whereby walkers, cyclists and horse-riders could follow a variety of trails that ran past old mines and along old disused tramways. This view shows the vanner house at Wheal Basset Stamps in September 2002. *Author*

Part of the vast Basset Mines complex was Merriot's Shaft, seen here well over a century ago. Of particular interest is the elevated conveying trestle between the whim house and the nearby stamps, which are visibly top fed. Again the remarkable superstructure around the granite mine buildings is impressive. The Great Flat Lode was one of the largest in Cornwall and it was vigorously exploited from the 1870s, resulting in a large number of mines in the area. *Cornish Studies Library*

Portreath (which they expanded to facilitate the export of ore from the family mines and to import coal and timber).

The family dates back to at least 1066 when one of the Bassets fought with William the Conqueror at Hastings. One Thomas Basset married the daughter of Dunstanville of Trehidy, and throughout the Middle Ages the family is mentioned in an immense variety of public and military contexts, holding posts such as Members of Parliament and Sheriffs of Cornwall.

Francis Basset started the Cornish Metal Company in 1782. This was a form of cartel, set up with the objective of purchasing all of the Cornish copper output, but it failed in 1792. Conditions for the workers in the mines were appalling and the wages were low. The miners could purchase food only by token at the mine-owner's stores, the value of which was determined by the owner. In 1785 there were 'food riots' and Francis Basset deputised 50 special constables to arrest the ring-leaders in dawn raids. Some were hung by the neck while others were deported. For his efforts Prime Minister Pitt made him Lord de Dunstanville in 1796. While these wealthy Cornish families provided employment and some aspects of welfare, they undoubtedly got richer at the expense of the poor. The huge 90-foot granite monument atop Carn Brea summit is dedicated to Lord de Dunstanville, but I doubt whether a starving miner of 1785 would have appreciated the gesture of Cornwall County Council.

The Great Flat Lode was one of the largest and most continuous ore-bearing geological structures south of the Carn Brea hill, between Redruth and Camborne. The lode was mined from the 1820s but hugely expanded at a later date. This entire south Great Flat Lode area is infested with old mine buildings, engine houses, stamping buildings and a plethora of old chimney stacks. By way of a small sample, these include Condurrow, dating back to 1818 but which later closed. It was reopened in 1830 and for many years produced about 1,750 tons of copper per annum before closing during the commodity crash of 1863. This stop/start pattern continued until 1914, when it closed for good. Another nearby mine called South Condurrow opened in 1850. It eventually closed in 1896 and in 1897 part of the mine was presented to the Camborne School of Mines and renamed King Edward Mine, under which it operates today as a learning centre and tourist attraction.

Other significant mines in the area include Wheal Grenville, East Wheal Grenville and Grenville United, the names relating to Baroness Grenville who in 1845 was the mineral lord for the mines. Nearly all of these mines had a stop/start history depending on the state of the commodity markets, before final closure. Wheal Uny can be traced back to the late 16th century when the area of 'Uni-Redruth' is referred to. However, the mine that emerged in 1824 was worked spasmodically until 1851, and between that date and 1893 it was hugely unsuccessful, making a profit only in the years 1872/3. After 40 years of loss-making it closed in 1893.

The remains in the Basset Mines area are quite remarkable in their scale and variety. This March 1997 view shows the wonderful complex around Marriot's Shaft at South Wheal Frances mine (SW 680389), named after Baroness Frances Basset, the daughter of Lord de Dunstanville (whose monument can be seen on the top of Carn Brea). Early workings here date back to the 1820s but the boom years were some 30 years later. By 1891 the mine had produced 68,000 tons of copper and 7,000 tons of tin. *Author*

Not all of the mines in the Basset complex were owned by the Basset family and many were leased out. The family also owned mines elsewhere in Cornwall. Those that carried a family name were Wheal Basset, East Wheal Basset, South Wheal Basset, West Wheal Basset, Basset Mines Ltd, South Wheal Frances and West Wheal Frances (Frances, Baroness Basset, was the daughter of the first Lord de Dunstanville). Wheal Basset in particular should be mentioned, as by 1720 it had raised £100,000 worth of tin with a huge profit for the family and the lessees. Between 1832 and 1880 the mine produced 128,000 tons of copper ore and by 1868 had yielded dividends of £300,000. The mine amalgamated with South Wheal Frances in 1896 to become Basset Mines Ltd, finally closing in 1918. It should be mentioned that an 18-inch-gauge tramway served much of the Basset Mines complex.

South Caradon

There was an impressive group of mines in the area just south of Caradon Hill, north of Liskeard. Copper was discovered in 1836 when some ore examples were extracted from the area and were found to be of good quality. However, raising the necessary finance to commence large-scale mining activities was hard, and it was only after 130 tons of ore were raised in 1837 that investors decided to take the plunge. Lodes were struck, shafts were sunk and rich deposits were found at several locations.

These discoveries started a copper-mining 'gold rush', and between 1837 and 1861 the small nearby village of St Cleer saw its population increase by 400%. There were similar increases at Crow's Nest, Tremar, Darite and other nearby villages. The scale of operations cannot be overstated and by 1863 there were 4,000 men, women and

Above: Although the majority of engine houses and mining remains are to be found in west Cornwall, there were other important centres, one of them being around Caradon Hill, north of Liskeard. Following the discovery of copper in 1836, South Caradon Mine (SX 265700) hugely expanded with many different shafts being driven down into Caradon Hill. Here we see some of the remains on 12 June 1934. The granite setts on the left are effectively the sleepers of the Liskeard & Caradon Railway to Minions and the Cheesewring, via the Gonamena incline that was worked between 1844 and 1877. *Author's collection*

children working in no fewer than 35 mines. The output from the South Caradon mines was enormous and the complex boasted a 3.4-mile internal tramway system. South Caradon alone, with a manpower complement of 650, produced 217,820 tons of ore between 1837 and 1885, valued at £1,750,000.

Much of this output needed to be transported to the head of the Liskeard & Looe Union Canal basin at Lamellion Bridge near Moorswater, and it was no surprise when, on 26 June 1843, Royal Assent was given to a Liskeard & Caradon Railway Act. Construction commenced and the line was partly opened in 1844 and throughout in March 1846. The line extended beyond South Caradon to Cheesewring Quarry and other mines to the north of Caradon Hill. At the opening the entire workforce were 'regaled with roast beef and strong beer'! In later years the railway was extended all the way around Caradon Hill. By 1857 the railway carried 30,000 tons or ore and granite per annum.

After one of the great crashes in world commodity prices the South Caradon mines began to suffer – output dropped dramatically and mines started to close. At the end of the 1870s South Caradon experienced its first trading loss, and by 1885 the mines had all closed. There was a brief resurgence in 1888 but effectively mining at South Caradon had finished. The railway could not meet its liabilities and a Receiver was appointed in 1886; it struggled on until the First World War.

Many of the old structures have crumbled away with the passage of time but there are still many remains of the railway and the mines to be seen in this fascinating area. First above the valley floor is Sump Shaft, and Jope's Shaft (SX 265698), where a 60-inch pumping engine was once employed. Further east there are remains at Rules and Holman's Shafts (SX 269699) and beyond that site is Kittows Shaft. Even though gorse and ferns cover most of the area where there was such frenetic mining activity 150 years ago, one can just about imagine the scene in those far-off days (see also pages 37/38).

Just north of Crow's Nest are the multifarious remains of the South Caradon Mine complex. Other mines in the immediate vicinity included West Caradon, Rules Shaft, Kittows Shaft and East Caradon; all were closed by 1885. From 1861 the bridge featured here once carried the Tokenbury branch line, which was extended all the way around Caradon Hill from 1877, when the Gonamena line was closed. Note the remains on the hill beneath the still extant bridge (SX 264697). *Author*

The north coast

Mine workings in the Land's End area date back many centuries and evidence has been found of tin streaming that pre-dates the Middle Ages. Also, in the early days, before sophisticated machinery was invented, the lodes that extended horizontally beneath the

Mines litter the north coast of Cornwall, particularly in the St Agnes area and between St Ives and St Just. One of the most interesting was Giew Mine (SX 501369), which was located on Trink Hill, and at Franks Shaft is an engine house that once accommodated a 50-inch engine (steam engines were always measured by the diameter of their cylinders). The mine was 217 fathoms deep (1,302 feet). The last attempt at tin extraction was by the St Ives Consolidated Mines Ltd company in 1907, when this view was taken. The mine was the only active tin producer in Cornwall during 1921/2 when it closed.
Cornish Studies Library

ground would come to an abrupt end or be 'out-cropped' on the steep cliffs along the north coast, providing easy access to early prospectors. However, it must be stated that copper and tin lodes are more usually near vertical rather than horizontal. On the north Cornish coast from Cape Cornwall, near St Just, to Perranporth, north of St Agnes, there is a rich choice of old mining sites to visit and photograph. What sets some of these old mines apart from those in the other mining districts of Cornwall is their close proximity to the sea and the fact that many of the mine workings once extended some distance under the ocean.

Although there are a number of engine houses located on cliffs above the sea on the south coast, there are some spectacular examples on the north coast, as illustrated here. These engine houses varied in size, which to a considerable extent depended on the size of steam engine that was housed within. The engines were normally measured by the diameter of the cylinder, which could range from 18 inches to a massive 100 inches. Their shape also varied slightly depending on their primary purpose, which could be for pumping, lifting or powering other machinery, for example in stamping or crushing ore. These engine houses were extremely robust and were mostly constructed of huge granite blocks, with wooden stairways and galleries. The superstructure had to bear a substantial weight as the steam engines and all of their component parts, including the massive iron beam, connecting rods and flywheels, weighed many tons (in the case of larger engines about 40 tons), and although beautifully balanced, when in motion other stresses had to be absorbed. Including the heavy granite structure and all of the machinery contained within, a large engine house could weigh some 2,400 tons.

Apart from the size of the engine, the speed at which it worked would affect performance. In wet weather the pump might be worked at more revolutions per minute, which would remove more water from the mine but use more coal. Generally the steam engines worked at low pressure and low 'revs'. About five strokes per minute was normal, but if necessary they could be regulated up to eight revolutions per minute. In an emergency or during very wet weather a pumping engine may have to be flogged at twice the normal speed, but having regard for the weakest part of the system, the complex rodding beneath the ground. Huge volumes of water could be moved, but rarely was it brought to the surface. Normally it was discharged via an adit, or horizontal shaft or tunnel, which had been driven through an adjacent hillside into a nearby river. Whim or lifting engines were generally smaller than pumping engines, and sometimes several whim engines could be located at a single mine. Stamping engines could operate up to 64 stamps, which crushed the ore to the required size for smelting. Quite often the engine houses were in groups above or immediately adjacent to the mine workings, although they can also be found singly.

The general site of the Botallack Mine is a 'must' for visitors to Cornwall. The setting above the cliffs is spectacular. Above the famous Crown Engine Houses there was an extensive mine layout that in 1865 included no fewer than 11 engine houses, employing in total 500 people. The upper site was reworked between 1907 and 1914 when an arsenic works was built. Remains such as this are just one of the many attractions at a location that is a paradise for industrial architecture fans. Note the sea through the archway and the granite stack topped with brick. *Author*

Levant Mine is an important north coast survivor. The mine workings extended for more than a mile beneath the sea bed and it was 2,100 feet deep, below adit level. It began operations as a copper mine in 1820 and later tin was also produced. The mine finally closed in 1935, having survived a number of financial crises. A total of 31 men died in a terrible disaster in 1919 when the 'man engine' (a series of ladders) collapsed. The site is now maintained by the National Trust. The 27-inch whim engine on the left at Skip Shaft was built by Harveys of Hayle in about 1840, but the pumping engine has gone from the empty house on the right. *Author*

In addition to engine houses there was normally a boiler house near to the engine house(s). Depending on the size of the engine, the boiler house could contain between one and six boilers to provide steam for the massive engine(s). Sometimes at smaller engine houses the boiler 'house' was nothing more than a lean-to attached to the main building. Little is left of the boiler houses because their granite blocks and roof slates have been pilfered for reuse elsewhere. To increase the draught and for ease of handling at higher levels, some of the many engine house stacks had their top third made of brick rather than granite. These extensions also helped combustion, necessary when cheaper, poor-quality coal was being used. Nearly all of the stacks were circular, rectangular examples being more commonly found at brickworks. All were susceptible to lightning strikes and most had earthed conductors attached to them.

One of the most impressive pair of engine houses is located on cliffs above the sea at Botallack Mine (SW 361337). Known as the Crown Engine Houses, they were saved from destruction by sympathetic restoration by the Carn Brea Mining Society in 1985. One housed a 30-inch pumping engine and the other a winding engine, or whim. From the mine building there was wooden staging that gave access to a famous diagonal shaft that descended under the sea for 1,360 feet. The operating statistics in 1865 were impressive, with a total of 500 staff and 11 steam engines working above the ground. The mine received Royal visits on two occasions in the Victorian era, but working finally petered out in 1895. An arsenic works was built and operated between 1907 and 1914. There is much to see at this splendid spacious location, which normally enjoys the right crowd but no crowding.

Along the coast from Botallack is Levant Mine (SW 368345). This is another mine where workings ran out beneath the sea for more than a mile. Work at Levant started in 1820 as a copper mine, but by 1852 tin was also being produced. A disaster in 1919 killed 31 miners when a 'man engine' (moveable ladders) collapsed, but the mine lasted for a further 11 years, closing in 1930. A 24-inch beam winding engine on the site, built by Harveys of Hayle, was saved from the scrapman in 1935 by the Cornish Engines Preservation Society, and is now steamed by members of the Trevithick Society; the site is managed by the National Trust. There is an adjacent pumping house that once contained a 45-inch steam engine, and a narrow-gauge tramway once operated around the mine. Nearby is a tall chimney with coursed brickwork that stands above an old compressor house.

A short distance to the east is Geevor mine (SW 375345), which is now the site of the Geevor Tin Mine Museum. Mine tours are offered and, although designed for tourists, it is possible to partake of a not totally convincing pseudo-underground 'mine walk'. The most interesting exhibits are the tin dressing mills and mining exhibits in old buildings. The mine worked from 1911 until 1986, at which time it was one of the very

The Crown Engines at Botallack Mine (SW 361337) were literally perched on a cliff edge, and a complex wooden superstructure was needed to access the Diagonal Shaft that descended 1,360 feet below sea level. Queen Victoria and Prince Albert visited the site in 1840, and in 1865 the Duke and Duchess of Cornwall (later King Edward VII and Queen Alexandra) descended into the workings. This wonderful old view dates back to 1890. The main work ceased in 1895 but some minor activity continued until the First World War. *Cornish Studies Library*

last working tin mines in Cornwall. The main shaft is called Victory Shaft, so named to commemorate the defeat of Germany in 1918, and there is a steel head frame above it. Overall the museum is well worth a visit.

To the east on the B3306 road to St Ives is Carn Galver tin mine (see p6), where two engine houses stand as silent sentinels. One of the buildings housed a 40-inch pumping engine and the other a 20-inch whim engine. Some restoration work has taken place to ensure that the buildings are in a state of arrested decay. The main shaft was some 780 feet in depth.

There are a large number of mines around St Agnes, but one worth special mention, if only because of its position halfway down a cliff between Chapel Porth and St Agnes Head at SW 700502, is the much photographed Wheal Coates. The mine was not particularly successful and comparatively little tin or copper was produced. It closed in 1889, although one later attempt was made at viable mining in about 1911. On top of the cliffs are winding and stamp engine houses and the main engine house is beside Towanroath Shaft. Again the National Trust has ensured that the shells of the buildings are saved for posterity and some tasteful restoration work has been undertaken. The nearby Wheal Kitty can be found at SW 725513 and the boiler house and horizontal winding house remain extant.

Although not on the coastline, one further mine worth mentioning and already referred to under the Mining section is East Wheal Rose lead mine (SW 839558), near St Newlyn East. The mine was for some years Cornwall's principal lead mine and large quantities were shipped for smelting. The massive engine house that survives today is not the original, but it does date back to 1885, when a massive 100-inch engine was installed in an attempt to revive the mine. The mine was extremely wet underground and between the years 1842 and 1850 the water removal rate increased from an impressive 736 to a whopping 1,102 gallons per minute! Over time shafts were sunk to the 160-fathom mark (almost 1,000 feet) in the search for better tin lodes. In the year 1846 there were 1,200 men, women and children working at the mine when heavy rainstorms caused flash floods, which poured into the mine. The pumping engines were adjusted for maximum revolutions but they could not cope and as a result 39 miners were drowned, a terrible tragedy for the local community.

The Crown Engines gradually crumbled away but thankfully they were tastefully restored in 1985 by the Carn Brea Mining Society (see cover picture). All restorations have now weathered so that they nicely blend into the landscape. The lower engine house once held a 30-inch pumping engine while the upper structure, on the right here, contained a 24-inch winding engine. A footpath leads down to the mines, and for the able-bodied the experience of not only the engine houses but the Atlantic waves crashing against the cliffs is one to be savoured. *Author*

In 1849 the Newquay Tramway opened and the first 30 tons of lead ore left the mine, horse-drawn by rail and bound for the harbour at Newquay. Sadly output was already diminishing and the quality of the ore was deteriorating; by 1853 production was a mere 20% of the 1845 peak. After some 'stop/start' activity the mine finally closed in 1885. The remains are best seen from the Lappa Valley Railway (see page 169).

Smelters

In order to separate the significant volumes of copper and tin from the mined ore, which contained rock and other substances, it was necessary to smelt it, a process that involved heating it to sufficiently high temperatures to liquidise and separate the copper, tin, lead or iron. Although early smelters in Cornwall were known as 'blowing houses', and were charcoal-fired, smelting on a large scale was by coal-fired furnaces. To provide the necessary heat huge amounts of coal were required, and as far as copper was concerned it was simply not cost-effective to bring the coal to the copper smelters and accordingly most of the ore mined was taken to South Wales for smelting (although in the early days Bristol was another important destination). Copper smelting was tried in Cornwall and a smelter at Copperhouse, near Hayle, was active from 1758 until 1820. Iron ore was also exported to South Wales for smelting but, as mentioned earlier, iron mining failed in Cornwall and it was never a high-volume industry.

Tin and lead smelting was a rather different story and there were smelters all over Cornwall. Some tin smelters were very old indeed, and the practice had been refined over the decades. In many cases the

When ore had been mined and crushed there was the smelting stage to be considered, to separate the metalliferous content. Although there was a large copper smelter at Hayle, in general terms all copper ore was sent from Cornwall to South Wales for smelting, where there was an abundant supply of coal. Smelting tin was a very different story and there were several tin smelters in the Royal Duchy. One of the largest was at Par, where the plant had a remarkable 248-foot-high stack. This local landmark was demolished in August 1907, some years after the plant closed, when fissures were discovered. Steeplejacks are about to remove 25 feet of brickwork prior to the structure being felled.
M. Dart collection

furnace bellows were worked by water-wheels. An early smelter was located at Calenick, near Truro, which opened way back in 1711 and continued smelting for a further 180 years. A bell and clock tower remain at the site at SW 821432. There were also many lead smelters in Cornwall, but mention must be made of the vast smelter at Par, adjacent to the harbour. Joseph Thomas Treffry had constructed the smelter to handle the output not only from his mines but also those of the Hawkins family, who owned East Wheal Rose, Cornwall's biggest lead producer for many years. The final smelter output was normally in the form of ingots. Even in those days it was known that smelting fumes were poisonous and Treffry had a colossal 248-foot chimney built, which was a local landmark for years; it was demolished in 1907 after fissures developed, long after closure of the works.

Foundries

It is now hard to imagine the immense amount of machinery that was in everyday use in the various Cornish mines. It was not just the huge beam engines with their pistons, cylinders, flywheels and connecting rods, but also the extensive range of other machinery used throughout the mining industry. A catalogue of mining equipment from the 19th century shows literally thousands of component parts, ranging from vast girders to nuts and bolts. The products of a foundry were not confined to mining and equipment – everything for shipping and transport to domestic use and the growing china clay industry was manufactured, using mainly cast and wrought iron.

Agricultural equipment, gear wheels for mills and mines, water-wheels and ancillary components, road overbridges, railway viaducts, boilers, pumps, edge tools, lamp posts, lintels and domestic appliances were all manufactured; at the peak mining period there were estimated to be some 60 foundries throughout Cornwall.

One of the most famous foundries was the Holman Brothers' example at Camborne. The company was to become one of the household names in Cornish mining for its mining equipment and drilling machinery. Latterly known as Holman-Compair, the

With a massive requirement for machinery in the mines and pits it is hardly surprising that significant foundries were established in Cornwall. In its heyday the most famous of all was Harveys of Hayle, which at its peak boasted almost 1,000 employees making everything from machinery parts and steam engines to ocean-going ships. The nearby rival Copperhouse Foundry was eventually acquired by Harveys and subsequently closed in 1867. The demolition of the old and long-abandoned Charlestown Foundry, near St Austell, in 2006/7 exposed its superb pitchback water-wheel, which once powered much of the machinery. *Author*

Messrs Holman Brothers of Camborne was a major supplier of mining equipment for decades. This family concern started in business in the town in 1801, but it would be the 1880s before their fame for the provision of mining and drilling equipment peaked. The company owned extensive factory premises, such as this now abandoned structure adjacent to Camborne railway station. During the 19th century there were some 60 foundries in Cornwall making everything from beam engines to water-wheels. *Author*

company name survived for more than 200 years, finally closing in 2003. The largest and most famous company was Harveys of Hayle. For well over a century the finest steam engines were manufactured by Harveys, many with a design input from Richard Trevithick who, incidentally, married John Harvey's daughter in 1897. The company's activities included all aspects of engineering and extended from mining to shipbuilding. Some of these ships weighed several thousand tons and some of the components cast in the foundry were in the 'heavy engineering' category. Harveys' steam engines were so efficient and well built that they were exported all over the world. In this context the wharves in Hayle Harbour were made good use of for exporting manufactured goods and importing raw materials; indeed, the company greatly extended the number of quays available.

Two other foundries worth mentioning are the Perran Wharf Foundry and the foundry of William West at St Blazey. The Perran Foundry (SW 776384) was established by the Fox family of Falmouth in 1791, yet another member of Cornwall's wealthy and influential mine-owning community. Many fine beam engines were produced at the foundry, but in 1858 the family sold the business to the Williams family, who continued until closure in 1879, following a severe downturn in the mining industry. At its peak the foundry employed 140 staff. The premises were later adapted for milling grain and later for other applications, before finally closing in 1986. The foundry was located on Restronguet Creek about 1 mile beyond Devoran, where remains survive. William West was the brother-in-law of Richard Trevithick and he opened a foundry at St Blazey in 1848. He, too, constructed some very fine engines, but perhaps the foundry was best known for the work undertaken for the Cornwall Minerals Railway, including the main bridge supports for Trenance Viaduct, just outside Newquay, and Carbis road bridge. West purchased St Austell foundry in 1856; he died in 1879 and the business was kept running by his sons until closure in 1891.

Quarries

There are many old abandoned granite and slate quarries throughout Cornwall, as well as scores of sites where these industries remain active, many of which are 'Sites of Special Scientific Interest'. This section illustrates both extant and extinct examples.

Right: There were many different types of quarrying in Cornwall. Granite, slate and roadstone were all contributors to the Cornish economy and as with other major industries there were scores of sites where quarrying took place. One of the evergreen problems with all commodities was shipping, and for these slates from Delabole the transportation to the beach was by horse and cart. The wooden ships were beached at high tide, loaded, then hopefully re-floated on the next high tide. This loading is taking place at Port Gaverne on the north Cornish coast. *Cornish Studies Library*

Above: This very rare postcard shows the Road Stone Company's siding between Helland and Tresarrett, on the Wenford Bridge branch line, which was open between 1911 and 1934. Standard gauge L&SWR, Southern Railway and Great Western Railway wagons are visible under the loader. In the foreground are some narrow-gauge tipplers that have conveyed the fine stone from the quarry (visible in the background across the River Camel) to the ramshackle-looking terminal. The photograph was taken by a Mr Whale of Blisland in the late 1920s. The concrete ramp at bottom right survives at SX 087723. *Author's collection*

Cheesewring

There is evidence of quarrying and mining around Caradon Hill going back many centuries but, as described in the South Caradon section (pp26/27), the pace of development in the area during the 19th century was breathtaking. Much of the land around Minions was owned by the Duchy of Cornwall and in 1839 it was one John Trethewey who sought permission to quarry granite at the Cheesewring. A substantial quarry was established and a number of buildings were constructed in the immediate area including a smithy and, from 1864, some workers' cottages. The Liskeard & Caradon Railway opened from 1844 and a connection was made into the quarry, alleviating transport problems and reducing costs. In 1842 it had been forecast that Cheesewring Quarry (SX 229724) would convey 8,000 tons of granite per annum by rail; the quarry provided the granite setts for the new railway. From 1846 granite was taken by rail to Moorswater, then by canal to Looe for shipment. The railway was extended to Looe in 1860.

The output from the quarry fell well short of expectations and in 1852 only a miserly 210 tons was conveyed on the railway, although some granite was still transported by cart. A change of ownership occurred and from 1854 tonnage increased dramatically, averaging about 4,000 tons per year until 1858, when it reached more than 6,500 tons. Production peaked in 1868 when the quarry was owned by Freeman & Sons, who had quarrying interests elsewhere. At this time about 100 staff were employed in the quarry. From that date there was a steady decline and the quarry closed between 1881 and 1884.

One of the most famous quarries in Cornwall was Cheesewring Quarry, near the 1,212-foot Caradon Hill, north of Liskeard. Thousands of tons of granite have been extracted from this location over past centuries although, in common with mining in the area, the 19th century was its most productive period. Cheesewring was rail-connected from 1844 (through to Moorswater in 1846) until the start of the First World War. In this 2004 scene, some 90 years after closure, a section of rail remains at the quarry entrance. A large number of granite setts in the area facilitate tracing the course of the old railway. *Author*

There was some upturn when Cheesewring's granite was used in the reconstruction of the viaducts on the old Cornwall Railway (by then the GWR). The quarry struggled on but by the First World War the railway had closed and the main chapter in Cheesewring Quarry's history had already been written. Cheesewring's granite dumps, some in the inner quarry, were disturbed in 1984 when much of the stone was plundered to reinforce Mountbatten Breakwater at Plymouth. There is still plenty to see in the area and a walk from the village of Minions to the old quarry is extremely rewarding.

Below: This remarkable old postcard shows an interesting piece of history from the turn of the 20th century. The 'Cornish Village' history card shows a view of Minions, then described on the card as 'Cheesewring Railway Village, Nr Liskeard'. 'Railways' had disappeared from the area by 1917. At the top centre of the card is Minions railway depot, and to left of the horse and cart is the alignment of the original Gonamena incline railway line, which had closed in 1877, 25 years earlier. *Author's collection*

Right: Just over 100 years later the scene at Minions is still recognisable, with the bend in the road, the left-hand wall and houses, the distant shop (and its upstairs windows) and the building on the right (note the window apertures) largely unchanged. This high-elevation village was the home for many miners in the mid to late 1800s and it is still worth exploring. There are easy walks to Cheesewring Quarry and the Hurlers stones. *Author*

De Lank Quarry near St Breward is now the only major granite quarry in Cornwall, although many other smaller quarries remain in operation. Over the decades De Lank has supplied quality granite for a number of prestigious buildings in London and its products have also been used in the construction of Cornish and other lighthouses. It was once rail-connected via an incline to Wenford Goods, but the line closed in the 1940s. In this incredible photographic postcard, posted in 1902, dressing floors and both standard and narrow gauge railways can be seen. *Author's collection*

De Lank

Taking its name from the De Lank river, which flows from the heights of Bodmin Moor into the River Camel, the quarry of the same name has been quarrying a form of igneous rock for generations. Known as Dimension Stone, the grey granite from the quarry has been used in some of the most famous buildings and monuments in the UK, such as the Princess Diana memorial fountain, the Eden Project 60-ton 'nut', Beachy Head and Eddystone lighthouses, and many important structures in the capital, especially the Thames bridges.

From the 1890s De Lank Quarry (SX 102752) was rail-connected, which had a profound effect on transportation. A standard gauge line from Wenford Bridge freight terminus crossed a local road and reached the quarry via a 1 in 8 cable-worked incline. Only two wagons at a time could be worked up or down the incline. There were a number of sidings and spurs at both the foot of the incline and in the quarry area. Until 1925 wagons were moved around the quarry by horse, but from that time until about 1950 a small locomotive was used. Large volumes of granite left the works by rail for shipment at Wadebridge. The incline closed about 1940 and was officially abandoned a decade later. Now owned by Ennstone Breedon Ltd, the 100-foot-deep quarry still produces a range of granite products from fine dressed stone to crushed rock, popularly known as aggregate.

Tintagel

Few of the thousands of visitors who come to Tintagel in the 21st century in order to see the remains of the cliff-top castle and its links with the tales of King Arthur, realise that well over a century earlier labourers had eked out a tough existence on the cliff faces quarrying slate. Working from ledges that were exposed to the weather, which in the winter months could be atrocious, these hardy folk quarried raw material and split the slates for shipment. In the absence of a local harbour, the slates were transported to a nearby cove by cart or by a cable and bucket pulley system, where small sailing ships would be simply beached, loaded and floated off on the next high tide. This could be a precarious business in high winds or if the ship was not perfectly positioned for the prevailing tide.

There were a number of cliff quarries all along the coast from Tintagel to Trebarwith, as well as examples further north towards Boscastle. The slates were not only used for roofing but also for gravestones, flooring slabs and by the construction industry, especially for lintels. As transportation systems gradually improved and the use of small wooden ships was discontinued, these cliff workings slowly petered out, especially once relatively nearby Delabole started producing huge volumes of slate.

In addition to granite, Cornwall has always been associated with slate quarrying. Apart from Delabole there were substantial works along the north-coast cliffs between Trebarwith, Tintagel and Boscastle until the early part of the last century. It is hard to imagine the hardship endured by the slate workers, especially being exposed to the elements in winter. In this tremendous view slate quarrymen can be seen splitting slates on the cliffs below Tintagel in Edwardian times.
Cornish Studies Library

Delabole

Although Wales has always been famous for its slate quarries, the largest quarry in England can be found at Delabole in Cornwall (SX 074835). As can be seen from the illustrations, the scale of operations is vast and by the late 19th century the main workings were some 400 feet deep. It is thought that slate quarrying has been active at Delabole for about 1,000 years, but certainly there were up to five separate quarries working in the area by the 16th century. These quarries were amalgamated in 1841 and the Old Delabole Slate Company was formed.

Some of the operating statistics were staggering, facilitated by the introduction of extensive mechanisation. Following the installation of a stationary steam engine in 1834 an internal railway system was provided from 1841 and over the years horse and steam power were used on the system, as well as cables on some of the steep inclines. The original

3-foot-gauge line was later converted to 1ft 11in. This was an extensive and complex system with narrow-gauge lines all over the works, serving most outbuildings and, via inclines, most of the quarry faces. The layout changed regularly to reflect quarry expansion and contraction. All of this slate had to be transported by horse and cart mostly to Port Gaverne, near Port Isaac, about 6 miles away along the 'Great Slate Road' (see page 36). When a small 60-ton-capacity sailing ship docked or beached it took 30 wagons and at least 90 horses to transport a ship-load of slates, broadly based on 2 tons per load and three horses per wagon. During the winter months the road was badly cut up and the

Right: Delabole (SX 074835) is without doubt the most famous slate quarry in the whole of England. Workings in the area date back to Elizabethan times but the current massive installation is in fact an amalgamated site of a large number of old small quarries. The distance from the surface to the bottom of the quarry is more than 400 feet and the site was served by narrow-gauge industrial railways and a standard-gauge siding for many years. Here a horse provides the shunting motive power and there are plenty of cables and pulley wheels to view. *Cornish Studies Library*

Below: This incredible photograph dates back to 1875 and shows the steep tramway incline down to the bottom of the quarry. Three workers are being cable-hauled up the incline while two further lines can be seen on the left.

Of special note is the impressive number of leats that have either been built or are in the course of construction to convey water to the water-wheels that powered much of the machinery. *Royal Institute of Cornwall*

AEROFILMS LTD., LONDON   DELABOLE SLATE QUARRIES, CORNWALL   NO. 45662
COPYRIGHT

This aerial view of the Delabole slate quarry complex gives an appreciation of the scale of operations. Tens of thousands of slates are stored in the open. Meandering in from Delabole station on the North Cornwall line, top left, is a siding to bring fuel, equipment and machinery into the quarry and to take slates and slate dust away to all parts of Britain. The caption on the back of this postcard view states: 'Quarries owned and worked by The Old Delabole Slate Co. Ltd., Delabole, Cornwall. The largest and oldest slate quarry in England. In continuous working since 1555.'
M. Dart collection

journey could take several hours. Without modern communications it is intriguing to speculate how the slate company knew precisely when a ship was arriving and when to dispatch the load from the quarry, especially in bad weather when ships could be sheltering in a port for days! Output increased and in 1859, for example, there were 1,000 employees at the quarry, which produced 120 tons of slate daily. The total output in the late Victorian period was phenomenal and, after the L&SWR's North Cornwall Railway 'main line' arrived in 1893, some 10,000 tons of slate per annum were conveyed by rail and the old horse-drawn wagons became part of Delabole's history.

In 1908 the company developed slate powder, sometimes irreverently referred to as slate dust. More recently, after 100 years of progress, this product has found a multitude of uses as inert mineral filler; slate powder and/or granules are used in bituminous mixers, asphaltic flooring, damp-proofing materials, fertiliser, filling compounds, insecticides, paints, printing inks, plastic, adhesives and rubber. The quarry remained profitable but there was increasing competition from abroad and from artificial lookalike materials. There was a long period of consolidation, which saw two World Wars come and go, but overall there was a decline in the industry. After incurring losses the Old Delabole Slate Company was liquidated in 1977 and, after a period of corporate ownership by Delabole Slate (1977) Ltd, the business was subject to a management buyout in 1999. There are now 40 employees, and just five experienced quarrymen produce 120 tons of slate per day, exactly the same as 1858 but with a fraction of the workforce. Technology has made all the difference and now diamond-wire saws cut 600-ton blocks from the quarry face, reducing waste to a minimum. The company is proud of the fact that 70% of the workforce live within walking distance of the quarry.

As can be seen from the accompanying photographs there has always been plenty of machinery in the quarry. In the early years power was produced by a number of large water-wheels, the water being brought to the quarry by leats and launders. As already mentioned, steam engines were also used for various purposes. There were overhead conveyor systems, or cableways, for removing the slate, and the internal railway was heavily used to deliver slates to the dressing sheds. Most of the finishing activities comprised splitting the slates, sawing them into required shapes and planing them. They were then stored in a vast open-air enclosure pending sale and transportation. Unfortunately the railway can play no further part in slate transportation because British Railways closed the North Cornwall Railway line completely in 1966 and the track and sidings were all subsequently lifted. For a short time, from 1967 until 1979, slate dust (powder) was taken by road from Delabole to Wadebridge, where is was loaded into railway wagons and taken down to the main line at Bodmin Road. However, during January 1979 the by then freight-only line also closed and the slate-by-rail era ended. The company has had no choice but to resort to road transport to convey its slate products.

The present quarry is 425 feet deep and its circumference is 1½ miles long. It is an impressive site and the operating company has entered the world of tourism by organising a daily tour for members of the public during the summer season at the modest cost of £2 per head. There is an interesting museum at the visitor centre and a shop where slate products can be purchased. In this building the centrepiece is one of the quarry locomotives, a 1925-built Motor Rail 4wDM four-wheeler identified as 'No 2'. The company is environmentally aware and operates in conjunction with the local authorities and in consultation with the local public at large on many issues.

Luxulyan

Luxulyan is an ancient parish with a fascinating history. In 200 years the population increased from 875 in 1801 to 1,371 in 2001, with a peak of 1,512 in 1841. Situated at the top of the lush Luxulyan Valley, the village gets its name from Luxulyanite, a rare type of Cornish granite, which was so attractive that it was chosen for the sarcophagus of the Duke of Wellington in St Paul's Cathedral. Granite

In order to connect the quarries, mines and pits of the Luxulyan and north Hensbarrow Downs area around Bugle with the harbour at Par, prominent landowner and businessman Joseph Thomas Treffry built a tramway from Ponts Mill to Colcerrow Quarry and Mollinis (Bugle), which opened in 1841 and 1844 respectively. The line included a 2,840-foot-long 1 in 9 incline plane, known as the Carmears Incline. This old checker's hut is at the top of the incline at SX 062569. Note the granite setts, defining the line of the old trackbed. *Author*

was to be an important commodity in the 19th-century development of Luxulyan and a number of quarries were worked in the surrounding area. The beauty of the countryside in and around the Luxulyan Valley, through which runs the River Par past rocky outcrops beneath mature deciduous trees, cannot be underestimated, and in 2006 it became a World Heritage Site.

Most of the major industrial and transport heritage in the Luxulyan area can be attributed to one man, industrialist, capitalist and entrepreneur Joseph Thomas Treffry (1782-1850). The Treffry estate included a wide range of mines, pits and quarries and he realised that the commercial success of many of these depended on a good transport system, not only for the minerals these sites produced but for the inbound raw materials, especially coal and timber. Although the problem will, inevitably, be mentioned many times in these pages, the Cornish roads in the late 18th century were appalling and, in terms of the Industrial Revolution that was about to occur in the county, not fit for purpose. The problem was that in most cases the various mines and pits were located some distance from the ports and harbours from which the minerals were shipped; some were on high ground or in deep valleys, and were not easily accessed. Even if conditions in the

Above: The entire Luxulyan Valley area is full of mining relics. At the bottom of the valley are the remains of the Ponts Mill clay driers and there is evidence of the old canal that ran down to Par from 1835 until replaced by the Treffry Tramway in 1855. Another remarkable survivor is the 2-foot-gauge tramway that connected a loading wharf at Ponts Mill with Prideaux Wood Clay Kiln. The abandoned track is seen here near Ponts Mill in 1995, at SX 073559. *Author*

Above: The most significant structure on the Treffry Tramway, and, for that matter, in this part of Cornwall, is the Treffry Viaduct, now a Scheduled Ancient Monument. Built between 1841 and 1844, this massive granite structure is 648 feet long and 98 feet high, comprising individual blocks that weigh between 5 and 6 tons. The viaduct carried the tramway across the Luxulyan Valley and also a leat to convey water to the water-wheel, which provided the power for the cable-worked incline and other machinery. Seen here in 1989, it is still possible to walk across the viaduct, at SX 056572.

This wonderful old scene shows the Treffry Tramway in situ on the Treffry Viaduct. Wagons were horse-drawn over this section of line, although both cable power and gravity were used elsewhere on the tramway. After the opening of the Cornwall Minerals Railway in 1874 traffic on the tramway rapidly dwindled, being confined to the occasional load of granite from the quarries located to the north-east of the viaduct. *Author's collection*

summer months were better, the loads still had to be carried by horses and mules or, slightly later in time, in unwieldy wooden wagons with a payload of between 2 and 4 tons.

Treffry was well aware that in west Cornwall and in South Wales in particular, tramways had begun to make an impression in the field of industrial transport. Both the Poldice Tramway of 1809 and the Redruth & Chasewater (*sic*) Railway of 1824/5 were in operation and Treffry was convinced that a tramway would be beneficial to his business interests, not only for the output from his mines and pits but for others who would gladly pay for a more efficient transportation system. His grand plan was to link the north and south coasts of Cornwall, thereby connecting the ports of Fowey and Par, which he had built on 35 acres of land he acquired in 1828, and Newquay, which he purchased in 1838. He was also keen to compete with the port of Charlestown, his main rival in the area, which was owned by the Rashleigh family. By the late 1830s Treffry had already built a canal from Par to Ponts Mill, at the foot of the Luxulyan Valley, where huge amounts of ore descended an incline plane from his vast Fowey Consuls mine. This mine once had six steam engines and 17 water-wheels, employing in 1836 1,680 workers, including 308 women and 315 children.

Various surveys were undertaken and eventually work commenced on the tramway. One major physical obstacle was the Luxulyan Valley, where a 2,840-foot incline plane with a 1 in 9 gradient would be necessary to gain 300 feet in height. Wagons would be hauled up the gradient, power being provided by a large water-wheel. This section of the tramway opened in 1841. At the top of the incline the tramway was worked by horses along a generally level alignment to granite quarries at Colcerrow and Carbeans with, from 1855, a reverse connection to Cairns Quarry.

In order to reach the higher ground around Bugle it was necessary to branch away from the original tramway and cross the valley by means of a massive ten-arch 648-foot-long, 98-foot-high granite viaduct, which took three years to build. The 5 to 6-ton granite blocks used in the construction came from Treffry's own quarries. Although now trackless, the Treffry Viaduct, now a Scheduled Ancient Monument, still also carries a major leat across the valley and stands as a fitting memorial to his vision. Visitors are rewarded by spectacular views of the valley and the Newquay branch line (SW 056572).

The tramway opened to Mollinis, near Bugle, in 1844, and for 30 years it performed a useful function, meeting many of the original objectives. It was extended to Par Harbour in 1855 and the canal was abandoned. Treffry died in 1850 without the envisaged connection to Newquay having been made. In 1873/4 the Cornwall Minerals Railway took over the various segments of tramway and built the standard gauge railway line from Fowey to Newquay, much of it on the alignment of the old tramway. Opened for freight in 1874, it would be 1876 before a passenger service was provided and Luxulyan station opened, although at that time and until 1905 it was known as Bridges. The CMR branch was re-routed up the Luxulyan Valley, avoiding Carmears incline, which gradually fell into

The wheelpit, a small part of the water-wheel and some rusting machinery have survived at the top of the Carmears Incline, and a visit to this tranquil area, set amongst deciduous trees, is highly recommended (sensible footwear is required). To avoid total destruction some renovation has taken place and safety railings have appeared in recent years. Here water from the leat is seen falling into the wheelpit in September 2006 (SX 062569). *Author*

disuse. The output from the quarries dried up in stages, from 1880 until about 1930. It is still possible to see the wheelpit, where the water-wheel and gear wheels were later used to grind china stone, and the leats at SX 062569 (see photograph). Luxulyan station is still open but all sidings and buildings have long disappeared (SX 047581).

At its southern end there was also another standard gauge line from Ponts Mill along the Luxulyan Valley at its lowest point, serving Rock Mill and Orchard Quarries, which opened between 1868 and 1870 and was used in the construction of the Newquay branch line. By the beginning of the 20th century the demand for granite was in steep decline and the tracks to these quarries and on the Carmears incline were all lifted for the war effort in about 1917. In the 1920s tracks were relaid along the valley floor to serve Trevanny Kiln, where china clay was dried; it is possible that the quarries were used to extract granite for construction of the kiln. The tracks were lifted in 1938 and later relaid, but only to the kiln. The Trevanny line was finally abandoned in 1967 but it is still possible to walk the route and to wander around the kiln, which has been fitted with safety railings for the purpose (SX 064565).

Explosives

The mining and quarrying industries were heavy users of explosives, including gunpowder and later dynamite. When the First World War started in 1914, Cornish explosive factories diversified into the field of ammunition, many having suffered from the downturn in mining. Explosives were used in increasing volumes in the late 18th and early 19th centuries when the Cornish mining boom commenced. These unstable substances had to be handled with great care and the installations tended to be located in remote areas such as secluded valleys, on cliff headlands or in sand dunes. Matters improved when the safety fuse was invented in 1831, a large fuse factory being established at Tuckingmill, near Camborne. In the early days the area between Truro and Falmouth, specifically around Ponsanooth, saw the birth of explosives factories in Cornwall, and from 1811 the largest works in Cornwall was the Kennall Gunpowder Company, located at Kennall Vale Gunpowder Mills (SW 751375). The works was enlarged in 1844 but the business moved to Hayle Towans in 1889 and became part of the National Explosives Company.

Of the many gunpowder works, Hayle Explosives Factory is worthy of mention (SW 578397). A railway siding served this works, which in part ran along the course of the old Hayle Railway. At the end of the 2-mile siding were exchange sidings, an engine shed, goods shed and an internal tramway. During the First World War there were 1,800 employees making dynamite, nitroglycerine, cordite and guncotton, but after the war the factory closed in about 1920. There was another gunpowder installation owned by C. M. Powder Co Ltd at Treamble, at the end of a branch line from Shepherds, but this was overwhelmed in size by the nearby Perranporth Explosive Works. Opened in 1891 on the cliff tops at Cligga Head (SW 737538) as the British & Colonial Explosives Company, the works was soon taken over by Nobel's Explosives and produced large volumes of dynamite. Work petered out in 1905 but there was a First World War revival before complete closure in about 1919. There are extensive and interesting ruins at the site as well as the remains of old mining activity – a visit is recommended. Until the 1960s explosives were also produced in East Cornwall at Trago Mills and by the East Cornwall Gunpowder Company at Herodsfoot.

Explosives and gunpowder works appeared on the Cornish scene in the 19th century but particularly after 1831 when the safety fuse was invented. Explosives were used widely in the mining and quarrying industries and in later years for military purposes. These utterly fascinating remains, seen here in 2007, can be found on Cligga Head, south of Perranporth, at SW 737538. They were once part of the British & Colonial Explosive Company's works, which opened in 1891 and closed in 1905, only to be revived during the First World War. The views from this rather spooky site are extraordinary.
Author

Textile mills

Based on the number of sheep in Cornwall it would not be unreasonable to expect that over the years the woollen and textile industry in the county would have been huge. Certainly there were a number of diverse establishments producing traditional woven textiles, knitwear, tweed and even carpets, but all were modest in size.

John Blamey's wool-combing mill at Lamellion Bridge was opened in the 1890s as the Duchy Tweed Mill. It was located adjacent to Coombe Junction station and, in times past, the Liskeard & Looe Union Canal, where there was an adequate supply of water. Lamellion corn mill was further upstream. In years past there had been disputes with the canal company, which was accused of misappropriating water to maintain levels in the canal. This large mill eventually closed and sadly was demolished in the 1970s. Blamey also owned The Wool Factory at Lowertown on the Gwennap River, where blankets were made in the early 19th century (SW 760406).

Kennall Vale lies between Stithians and Ponsanooth and it was estimated that there were up to 50 water-wheels revolving there in the 19th century. A last woollen factory existed at Ponsanooth Mills and there were other smaller mills in the area. All ceased several decades ago, although it was 1950 before the last wheel fell silent.

One of the best-known garment-manufacturing companies was pioneered by a lady who was popularly known as 'Madame Hawke'. In 1905 Mme Hawke's husband died, leaving her with six children. She started a clothes shop business in Newquay and made the garments herself by the use of a hand knitting machine. She sent samples of her work to Debenhams, which agreed to take her total output. She grew the business and moved to larger premises. During the First World War the Drake family took over and formed the Newquay Knitting Company, which at its height had 450 employees. Factories opened were the Newquay Knitting Company, Trinity Works, F. C. Hawke & Sons, Hope Knitting Company, Blystra Knitting Company, The North Cornwall Knitting Company, Oakleigh Hosiery Company and the West End Knitting Company. The Madame Hawke name is still in use, but there was a decline in the industry due to cheap foreign imports and, after being taken over by Messrs Abbot & Scaddon Ltd in 1961, the main factory in Crantock Street closed in the late 1960s. It has now been converted into houses and retirement homes.

Although Cornwall has always had plenty of sheep, its woollen textile industry was on a relatively small scale. A large woollen mill at Ponsanooth employing about 90 people was in operation until the early 20th century and there were several clothing manufacturers in Newquay. One of the larger wool-combing mills was John Blamey's establishment, which was located adjacent to Coombe Junction on the Looe branch (SX 239635), seen here in 1922. It was opened as the Duchy Tweed Mill in 1890 but sadly the building has been demolished in recent years. *Author's collection*

Windmills

With the rich selection of long-abandoned mine buildings in Cornwall it seems strange that there is not considerably more evidence of windmills in the county than presently exists. What is known is that way back in the 12th century there were a number of post-mills at work utilising the strong 'southwesters' that blow in off the Atlantic. Also, historical records indicate that there were more than 60 windmill sites identified throughout the county, used mostly for the conventional function of grinding corn. Surprisingly there are fewer than half a dozen sites where windmill remains of substance exist today. These survivors were all tower-mills and are located at Treffry Mill, Fowey, Mount Herman Mill at Landewednack, Empacombe Mill at Maker, Carlyon Mill near St Minver, and Trevone Mill at the village of the same name.

Of these remains, at Carlyon Hill windmill (SW 958754) there is a sail-less 30-foot tower in the middle of a field on top of a hill overlooking the Camel estuary. There was a mill shown on the same site in 1690. It seems that the surviving structure has not seen use for more than a century and a half. Trevone Mill is located on the other side of the River Camel at SW 896749, about a mile inland. Maker windmill is in the south-eastern corner of Cornwall and overlooks the Hamoaze part of the Tamar estuary. The most southerly windmill in the UK was Landewendack on the Lizard Peninsula; as with Carlyon Hill, the mill site pre-dates 1690, and it ceased working about 1827.

One of the reasons for the relative lack of windmills in Cornwall was the widespread use of water-wheels, which utilised the many rivers and streams running off the high ground and down to the sea. Furthermore the Cornish had the technical ability to divert watercourses via leats and launders to power machinery in mills that were not located on or near a natural watercourse. This machinery could include millstones, sawmills, various pumps and even threshers. Also, except for particularly dry summers, the availability of power from water was more reliable than wind.

Finally, as an amusing aside, during World War 2 a number of dummy windmills were erected to confuse the Luftwaffe in locating the site of RAF Predannack near Mullion.

Whereas water-wheels could be found in abundance in the County of Cornwall, windmills were used far less frequently. In fact, of more than 60 known sites there are only about half a dozen locations in the county where significant remains can still be located (see text). Seemingly protected by bovines, the remains of the 30-foot-high hilltop Carlyon Hill windmill (SW 958754), seen here in 2007, overlook the Camel estuary. Records show that a mill existed at this location in 1690 and it is likely to have been in action for the following century and a half. *Author*

Water-wheels

It is now hard to imagine Cornish industry operating without electricity, gas, steam power or the internal combustion engine. However, more than two centuries ago wind and water were the primary sources of power at one end of the scale, with single candles attached to miners' hats to provide light underground at the other end.

The practice of harnessing wind power (see the previous section) and water power, in particular to grind corn, goes back many centuries and there is plenty of evidence to demonstrate that the early residents of Cornwall were proficient in these techniques. Numerous examples exist in Cornwall where, in areas where fast-running streams ran down often narrow valleys, there were dozens of water-wheels within a short distance of each other, all harnessing what was basically the same water supply. The presence of water was so important that property deeds and legal agreements dating back to the 14th century contain clauses referring to water rights and the granting of water courses.

In many mining areas there were no natural streams or rivers that could be exploited by industry, or they were in the wrong place or at an unworkable level. In such cases great ingenuity was shown in either redirecting streams to the point of application or, more usually, by constructing leats (artificial watercourses), sometimes over quite lengthy distances. In some areas, such as the Luxulyan Valley, there was a network of leats that served a multitude of industrial purposes. These leats could comprise either trenches in the ground or long wooden troughs, especially when water needed to be carried above the ground and over valleys or uneven land. This water would feed water-wheels. In the case of small mills these were attached to the main building, with gears on a central axle driving a range of machinery. Alternatively a crank was attached to the wheel, with rodding driving the relevant machinery. One early application was to power stamping machinery, vertical metal rods that were raised and lowered by cams in order to crush ore.

Before steam power was in general use, water-wheels were used in an almost infinite number of applications, for example for pumping water out of mines, powering conveyors and sawmills, in corn and grist mills, in textile mills, raising stone out of quarries, crushing clay at brickworks, and powering agricultural machinery. The wheels were either 'overshot',

Coombe Mill

The earliest use for water-wheels was conventional corn-grinding, but wider applications were soon introduced and provided an essential form of power for a wide range of industrial installations. Many such sites were located in valleys where there were often fast-flowing streams. Alternatively water-wheels were positioned at major works sites, where water was either piped or carried along leats and launders to the site of the wheel. This fine postcard shows Coombe Mill near Bude, which was latterly used by a timber merchant. *Author's collection*

with the water being delivered at the top of the wheel before capture, or 'pitchback', where the wheel moved in the opposite direction from an overshot example. They also varied in size, with a diameter of up to 40 feet being commonplace.

Once steam power arrived the use of water-wheels in the mines rapidly diminished. In many mills oil and gas engines replaced the wheels, and much later electric motors were used, which all improved reliability and were generally cost-effective. Gradually the water-wheels stopped turning and many were removed for their scrap value. It is said that the last water-wheel in everyday use lasted until the 1960s, and since then a handful have been restored to working condition. A good example is at the Wheal Martyn China Clay Museum at St Austell (SX 005554).

Right: These two fantastic pitchback water-wheels, seen over a century ago at Delabole slate quarry, are approximately 40 feet in diameter and were used to power quarry equipment. They are being supplied with water via launders (leats carried on elevated trestles), which are clearly visible. The narrow-gauge tramway lines and trucks are also of interest. *Royal Institute of Cornwall*

Below: Dressing floors were areas where large lumps of ore were graded manually by ladies, who were known as 'bal maidens'. The material was then transported to crushers or stamps and finally processed in 'buddles' to separate prime metals from waste rock before the former was smelted. A fine water-wheel dominates this scene at Wheal Frances, near Troon, as ladies, men and boys pose for the Victorian cameraman. *Cornish Studies Library*

Brickworks

Bricks and pipes have traditionally been made of clay of a suitable quality, but in Cornwall bricks have not only been made of clay but also of decomposed elvan stone (granite and rhyolite) and even certain types of inferior china clay, mixed with appropriate volumes of sand to produce bricks and building blocks. With the many boilers located around the mining and china clay installations of Cornwall there was a great demand for firebricks as well as building bricks, and to meet this need a number of mainly small brickworks were established. In general terms Cornish brickworks started to be established about 1850 and a few continued until the mid-1930s. Although most of the output was used domestically, in Cornwall and Devon some of the firebrick output was exported. The scale of operations was impressive with, for example, the Tamar Brickworks & Potteries Company covering 4½ acres of ground with a weekly output capacity of 80,000 firebricks. The main brick-making areas in Cornwall were above the River Tamar at Gunnislake, at Hingston Down in east Cornwall and around china clay country at Carbis, Par Harbour and at Trerice on the old Retew branch line, south of St Dennis Junction and near St Columb Road station, in mid-Cornwall. Many of these brickworks had their own narrow-gauge tramway systems. There was another substantial firebrick works in the mining area at St Day; the St Day Fire Brick & Clay Company was active for more than half a century before its demise in 1912. There were also small works dotted about the county, wherever there was a source of suitable raw material.

All of the larger brickworks were well placed in transportation terms, with the Par works being immediately adjacent to the harbour and railway line, Carbis being at the end of the Carbis Wharf branch from Bugle, and the Tamar companies delivering their products to Calstock Quay on the relatively nearby river. The Carbis and Carkeet brickworks featured in the illustrations are fascinating and well worth a visit, a common feature being the square brick chimneys, which stand in contrast to the more usual circular granite stacks of the mines and clay dries. There were many different types of brick kiln and the surviving examples at the above sites are either 'beehive' kilns or circular down-draught kilns. Most of these brickworks impressed the name of their particular works in each brick and there are active brick collectors on the lookout for rarer examples!

One of the saddest sights is where fine machinery from centuries past, having stood idle for decades, simply rusts away. Caught on film just in the nick of time is this water-wheel and associated gear wheels located at Carbis Brickworks (SX 001595), between Bugle and Roche, in September 2007. Located over a stream that runs down from high moorland south of Roche Rock, the wheel was used to drive 'pug', which crushed clay prior to the brick-making process. *Author*

In recent years some of the old china clay spoil tips have been re-excavated to recover the mica waste contained therein. A number of uses have been identified for this material in the building industry, and it has been widely used in the manufacture of building blocks (which resemble the old-style 'breeze blocks'). Gradually some of these old tips are disappearing as the waste of yesteryear is extracted, and a recent development has been the shipment of dedicated trainloads of this spoil from a rail-connected loading point at Burngullow, on the southern rim of clay country. There are encouraging signs that this traffic could increase as quickly as the output from the traditional brickworks decreased.

Above: Wherever a suitable source of clay was identified, a brickworks was often established. Although granite was the most common building material readily available in the county, bricks produced in Cornwall were also used in the building trade for a variety of structures. Often there was a pipeworks within the brickworks complex. One of the most remarkable but remote sites is Carkeet Brickworks (SX 219732), located by the infant River Fowey on Bodmin Moor and disused for more than a century. In September 2007 a decorative stack and drying shed survived, while on the left is a circular downdraught kiln. The works was in operation in about 1900. *Author*

Right: Very few brickworks survive, but Carbis Brickworks is one of them. The three round 'beehive' kilns were near collapse and in recent times two have been topped-off and one has had the full beehive brickwork restored, as seen here in October 2007. The main stack is unusual in that it is square and, not surprisingly, made of brick, in contrast to the granite stack of Great Wheal Prosper Clay Kiln on the left. *Author*

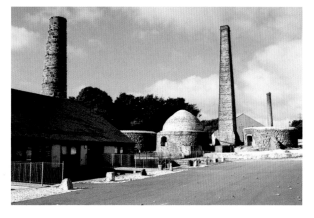

China Clay

China clay is produced from kaolinite or decomposed granite. Although the first discovery is attributed to the Chinese in the 7th century, there is evidence that the substance was used in pottery 1,000 years before Christ. In the long term its discovery in Cornwall was to be more significant than a century of copper and tin mining. The discoverer was William Cookworthy, a chemist from Plymouth, who in 1746 discovered some small deposits around Tregonning Hill to the west of Helston. More importantly, he found large deposits two years later at St Stephen-in-Brannel to the west of St Austell. It transpired that the entire Hensbarrow Down area, covering some 180 square kilometres, was rich in china clay and china stone, which is still being extracted.

It took some time for the trade to develop. At the end of the 18th and the beginning of the 19th centuries the mining of tin and later copper was all-important in Cornwall, while china clay extraction was, at that time, on a small scale. Some of the pits produced in a year less china clay than could be found in a single trainload today. Nevertheless, the industry was to become world-renowned and the timing of its development, particularly from the late 1870s, was almost perfect in replacing mining as Cornwall's major employer.

In the early days it was the potters around Stoke-on-Trent who took out leases on china clay pits because they were the primary customers of what is called Cornwall's 'white gold'. The main clay-drying process originally took place in what were called 'air dries', but the faster and more efficient method of pan-drying gradually took over from about 1845. Extracted clay would flow in a clay stream and by various processes be separated from earth, rock and sand before being deposited in a settling tank. The settled clay would be pressed to reduce the moisture content, then dried by warm air from a boiler at one end of the clay-drying building passing beneath it, with smoke and gases being emitted from a chimney at the other end. The dried clay would then be dropped into a 'linhay' and from there loaded into small horse-drawn wagons or, at many sites, into railway or tramway wagons and transported to the nearest suitable harbour for shipment. Prior to 1859 there

Along with its 19th-century mining activities, Cornwall has a lasting association with the china clay industry. From William Cookworthy's discoveries at Tregonning Hill near Helston in 1746 and at St Stephen-in-Brannel, near St Austell, in 1748, the production of china clay (and china stone) in Cornwall has been continuous. The history of china clay can be traced at the Wheal Martyn China Clay Museum near St Austell (SX 005554). This view shows the entrance in March 2007 and the sculptures feature everybody from the worker and the 'bal maiden' to the Shipping Captain. *Author*

Clay pits varied enormously in size. This relatively small installation is Single Rose China Clay Pit, photographed in about 1910. The hillside having been blasted by water through high-pressure monitors and with the first stage of china clay separation having commenced, workers can be seen near the clay stream filling a wagon with overburden (waste). Note the diminutive turntables for the hand-propelled narrow-gauge wagons. *Cornish Studies Library*

was no rail connection with the rest of the UK and the total output was conveyed in small wooden sailing ships. For well over a century from 1791, ports at Charlestown, Pentewan, Par, Newquay and Fowey were developed to cater for the china clay industry. Many other ports were also used but volumes were small.

The railway system serving the china clay industry also expanded and a complete network of branch lines and sidings grew up around the industry between 1829, when the Pentewan Railway opened, and 1920, when the Trenance Valley or 'Bojea' line was ready for service. The former line closed in 1918, but a rationalisation of the network, which started in 1964, has continued ever since. However, even in the 21st century well over a million tons of china clay is still moved by rail every year.

By 1913 there were 5,000 Cornishmen working in the china clay industry, which was booming. The complete Cornish landscape north of St Austell changed as pits became more widespread and deeper – the land was said to resemble a moonscape. Over the years there have been large-scale amalgamations in the industry and eventually more than 100 companies would be absorbed by the huge English China Clays Company (ECCI) before it, too, was taken over. To give but a single example of the scale of production and transportation, during 1985 1.4 million tons of china clay were

The author photographed this remarkable 'moonscape' at Virginia Clay Works in June 1989. It is difficult to grasp the scale of operations, but major buildings are dwarfed by the sheer size of the pit. In the upper centre of this view three monitors blast the hillside while roadways and tramways provide access to all parts of the site. For every ton of china clay recovered it is necessary to remove 8 tons of material, and great piles of waste and mica build up to produce massive spoil tips, which over time are seeded and in due course hide their man-made origins. *Author*

exported through Fowey Docks alone! Drying china clay in pan dries required huge amounts of coal to be imported, which was expensive. Consequently, over time, two major changes occurred: the employment of new mechanical drying and milling processes using modern and clean energy sources, and an improvement in pipeline technology, whereby china clay in liquid slurry form would be piped several miles to a central drying plant located at Par Harbour. This was the death knell for the pan driers; the last coal-fired installation at Great Wheal Prosper, owned by the Goonvean & Rostowrack China Clay Company, closed in 1989.

Right: Although the majority of china clay was found in and around Hensbarrow Downs, north and north-west of St Austell, there have been discoveries in other areas, such as Bodmin Moor and in the far South West. Two of these now abandoned pits were Balleswidden and Leswidden, between Penzance and St Just. This view shows part of the extensive remains at SW 391312. Much of the china clay/stone was transported by road to the docks at Penzance. *Author*

Below: Over the years technology has changed substantially and this has affected many aspects of the china clay industry. With the arrival of electricity and gas the old coal-fired pan kilns were phased out, the last such installation at Carbis Wharf having ceased production in 1989. Also the development of pipeline technology has resulted in china clay in slurry form being piped many miles for drying. One of the sites of yesteryear is Carloggas on the Drinnick Mill complex, now sadly abandoned. As with many sites, this is on private land at SW 957552. *Author*

Above: Over the years a large number of clay-drying plants have been rail-connected to facilitate the transportation of Cornwall's 'white gold' to customers worldwide. At some plants operations are on such a scale that a domestic shunting locomotive is permanently in residence. Such was the case at Rocks by Goonbarrow Junction, and the Blackpool complex at Burngullow. On 14 September 2003 Rolls Royce/Sentinel No P403D *Denise* of 1960 manufacture is seen at Blackpool covered in china clay dust. *M. Dart*

Above: To give some impression of scale, a new freight flow commenced during 1989 whereby china clay slurry was transported from the Blackpool loading point at Burngullow to Irvine in Scotland for use in paper-making. Within the first 10 years of operation a grand total of 1 million tonnes of china clay slurry had been transported by rail! On this September day in 2004 one of the modern North American-built new-generation freight locomotives, 3,200hp computer-controlled No 66115, leaves the vast Imerys works at the start of its long journey north. *Author*

Uses for china clay have expanded enormously since the early days. It is now used as a filler in paper production, for coating high-quality paper, and in the manufacture of ceramics, rubber, paints and polymers, plastics, fertilisers, insecticides, pharmaceuticals and medicines, leather and textiles. Different grades of china clay are used in each of these applications. There has always been competition from other countries and in recent years there have been worrying signs that lower labour costs elsewhere in the world would impact on the Cornish output. In 1999 ECCI was taken over by the French company Imerys, which is responsive to world commodity prices and international business economics. Presently about 2,500 staff are employed in the industry, which in terms of exports generates income in excess of £220 million per annum.

In addition to the large present-day clay production sites there are remains of the industry to be seen all over Cornwall. The main visual evidence is the large conical spoil tips of old. Over the years many have self-seeded and are now covered in foliage. More modern tips are significantly larger and the waste materials have been graded and deliberately seeded to blend in with the landscape, forming man-made mountains. There are also huge, mostly water-filled, pits at many locations, and some of the old pan dries and disused engine houses, both with their distinctive stacks, are scattered about clay country. As already described, a number of old ports are also worth a visit, but for an overall appreciation of the industry a visit to the Wheal Martyn China Clay Museum near St Austell is highly recommended.

Carbis Wharf

The delightfully named Great Wheal Prosper clay kiln at Carbis Wharf (SX 002596) is featured here because it was the last coal-fired pan kiln in Cornwall to dry china clay; it was also the very last to be rail-served. It was owned by the Goonvean & Rostowrack China Clay Company and even now, some 20 years after closure, there is still plenty to see at the site.

As already mentioned, the last old-fashioned coal-fired clay-drying installation, owned by the Goonvean & Rostowrack China Clay Company, was Great Wheal Prosper at Carbis Wharf. The railway line was opened in 1874 by the Cornwall Minerals Railway and closed in 1989. With Roche Rock in the right background and with Carbis Brickworks behind, No 37207 *William Cookworthy*, appropriately carrying the Cornish Railways insignia, leaves the old works in the rain during October 1985. *Author*

With an average of only a single wagon per month leaving Carbis Wharf for Armitage Shanks in Scotland, and with a new Goonvean pipeline to the Trelavour loading point in operation, the site was doomed, with both the clay-drying plant and the brickworks being closed permanently. Thieves removed many of the roof slates from the Grade II-listed building, but happily the site was acquired by Colin and Anne Coad, who restored and converted the site for residential use, 'B&B' and holiday lets. This is how the complex looked in September 2006, a tribute to all concerned. *Author*

Over the decades there have been many clay-drying plants in the Bugle area. In addition to Great Wheal Prosper there was Rosemellyn, West Goonbarrow, Great Beam, Wheal Rose, Wheal Martin and others. However, between 1948 and 1989 they all closed as new drying and production methods were introduced and new clay pits were opened. The event that had the greatest influence in the area was the arrival of the Cornwall Minerals Railway in 1874. An entrepreneur from London called William Richardson Roebuck had taken over the old standard-gauge Treffry Tramways, which since 1844 had served Bugle, terminating at nearby Mollinis. However, Roebuck linked Par with Fowey by rail and also bridged the gap between Mollinis and St Dennis Junction, giving direct access from Fowey to Newquay, with additional branches serving the china clay and china stone industries.

One of these branches was from Bugle to Carbis Wharf. The arrival of the railway was welcomed by the owners of the china clay pits and in many cases they gave the necessary land to the CMR. Construction was relatively straightforward, although there were two minor road crossings, and a road bridge had to be constructed at Carbis, the main support for which was cast in the foundry of William West of St Blazey. The mile-long single-track branch was built on level ground, but towards the end of the line there was a gradient of 1 in 44. It served both Rosemellyn and, from 1912, West Goonbarrow kilns. At Carbis Wharf two sidings were provided, one serving the clay dries and the other a wharf, for general goods use. There was never any provision, or space, for a run-round loop, and throughout the 115-year history of the line trains were always propelled from Bugle.

The track was modified at Carbis in 1901 when the length of the two sidings was doubled, and a catch point on the 1 in 44 gradient was relocated from one side of Carbis bridge to the other. At its peak, traffic volumes on the Carbis Wharf branch were considerable and some trains were double headed by two 0-6-0 pannier tank steam locomotives. As was usual on such lines, coal for the pan dries was an important source of inbound rail traffic. There were trains at least daily, although this would radically change during the 1980s. The line was an essential part of the china clay rail network, but once Rosemellyn closed in 1948 and West Goonbarrow ceased drying china clay in about 1963 there was a significant decline in traffic. Rationalisation on the Newquay branch at Bugle in 1973 saw the signal box there abolished, and from that time Carbis Wharf was treated as a single-line siding from Goonbarrow Junction.

Gradually traffic declined, and by the 1970s the small wooden-bodied wagons were no longer loaded at Carbis. Only a single customer latterly used the china clay from Great Wheal Prosper, the Armitage Shanks company based in Scotland, in the manufacture of bathroom furniture. The clay was conveyed in one of the then new 80-tonne 'Tiger' wagons. To prevent cross-contamination, only a dedicated vehicle was used, No TRL 11600, which worked from Cornwall to Scotland and back, with a loading/unloading circuit taking about three weeks to complete, which was of course the same as the frequency of the train service on the branch. By 1989 the track was in appalling condition and a new pipeline had been opened to Goonvean's Trelavour works; consequently the Carbis branch sadly closed. A decade later the Grade II-listed building was saved for posterity and tastefully converted to residential, 'B&B' and holiday let accommodation by Colin and Anne Coad.

Par Harbour

The Treffry family of Place, Fowey, had extensive landholdings in Cornwall and owned a considerable number of mines and china clay pits, including the vast Fowey Consuls mines. The family also had substantial business interests in Fowey, including part of the docks, and Joseph Thomas Treffry wanted to link Fowey with the Par area by tramway and extend it from the south coast to the north coast. However, the rival Rashleigh family, who owned some of the land between Par and Fowey, were against Treffry's plans, fearing they would damage trade at their harbour at Charlestown. As a railway to Fowey ceased to be an option, Treffry acquired 35 acres of land at Par in order to build a large tidal harbour for the shipment of ore, granite, clay and other merchandise and the importation of coal, lime, timber and fertiliser. Detailed plans were drawn up in 1828 and these included a vast 1,200-foot breakwater to the south and west of the harbour to shelter it from south-westerly gales. Although not finished until 1840, steady progress was made and by 1833 Par received its first commercial sailing vessel. In the same year Treffry opened a canal from Par to Ponts Mill, where an inclined plane lowered the ore from the Fowey Consuls mine complex.

Work started on his tramway from Ponts Mill and up the Carmears Incline in the Luxulyan Valley in 1839, and the first stage, to some granite quarries above Luxulyan, opened in 1841. This was extended to Mollinis, near Bugle, in 1844, and in 1855 the tramway was extended to Par Harbour and the 2-mile-long canal closed. Within a decade there was another depression in the mining industry and output dropped significantly. It must have been a great shock locally when in 1867 Fowey Consuls closed. However, the china clay business was picking up and Par proved its commercial worth with 15,000 tons

Above: Par Harbour was the brainchild of Joseph Thomas Treffry, who decided that to compete with Charlestown, owned by the rival Rashleigh family, he needed to create his own export outlet. In 1828 plans were drawn up for a completely artificial harbour occupying some 35 acres. The harbour would be tidal and protected by a 1,200-foot breakwater. It received its first ship in 1833. With eight sailing ships and two steamers in view, this circa 1902 illustration shows railway wagons and horse-drawn carts all over the place, with the GWR main line in the foreground. *M. Dart collection*

Above: Par Harbour was for years the busiest port in the whole of Cornwall, with china clay products being the major export until 2008. It was mostly coasters that used the port, conveying their cargo to British and nearer European ports. Larger vessels were, and still are, loaded at the deep-water port of Fowey. Here, on 31 August 1954, the good ship *Simultaneity* is loaded with china clay, while to the right is Bagnall 0-4-0ST *Alfred*, one of the diminutive steam locomotives with cut-down cabs. *Author's collection*

The main centralised clay-drying plant in Cornwall is located at Par Harbour, where most of the clay arrives via pipeline. The steam from the chimneys is emitted 24 hours a day, seven days a week. Significant numbers of lorries are also loaded, and they take dried china clay to Fowey via a road that once formed the trackbed of the old St Blazey to Fowey branch line, which closed in 1968. This view of the plant was taken from Par Beach in September 2002. *Author*

of china clay being shipped in 1855, 30,000 tons in 1860, 44,000 tons in 1865 and by 1870 a whopping 52,000 tons. There was something of a recession in the mid-1870s, but within a decade 85,000 tons of china clay passed through Par Harbour.

Treffry died in 1850 and in 1859 the Cornwall Railway's broad gauge main line had been opened from Plymouth to Truro. The Cornwall Minerals Railway had taken over the Treffry Tramways in 1873/4 and had built a new line from Par (or more accurately St Blazey) to Fowey via the longest railway tunnel in Cornwall, Pinnock Tunnel, 1,173 yards. Despite rail access to the rest of the UK and a direct line to the deep-water harbour at Fowey, the figures shipped from Par continued to be impressive. In Victorian times there was a large lead smelter at Par and a brickworks. The harbour site also included a timber yard, a saw mill, a flour mill and, under the main line to the north, a siding serving the Par Moor complex of pan kiln clay driers. Gradually the old wooden 30-ton to 250-ton sailing ships disappeared from the scene, replaced by steamships, followed in more recent times by coastal motor vessels with a displacement of about 2,000 tons. During 2008 all china clay shipping (as distinct from processing) was, surprisingly, transferred to Fowey.

In the 20th century ECCI built a bulk clay store and a huge centralised clay-drying plant at Par, to which much of Cornwall's output was piped in slurry form. The harbour complex was worked by the clay company's own steam shunting locomotives with cut-down cabs, due to a low bridge. There was also a hotchpotch of internal-combustion-engined shunters over the years, and road-going tractors have regularly been used to move wagons. In 1961 ECCI modernised and enlarged the port, providing a total of 10 berths for coaster-sized vessels. Larger vessels were handled at Carne Point, Fowey. ECCI purchased Par Harbour outright in 1964 and in the calendar year 1965 1,500 vessels used the port. In 1968 the old railway line from Par Bridge to Fowey was closed and converted

Just along the coast from Par is Charlestown. Founded by Charles Rashleigh, after whom the port is named, it was also built to cater for ever-increasing volumes of minerals from the mines and pits. Much of the surrounding hillsides had to be excavated to create this artificial port, and between 1790 and 1800 an entire village was built around the harbour area. A large pair of lock gates were provided to retain the water level within the harbour area, which could accommodate ships of around 300 tons. In this 2007 view a sailing ship is visible behind the enlarged lock gates, a single clay loading chute remains and the stack of the closed Lower Charlestown Clay Driers can be seen centre background. *Author*

to a private road for the exclusive use of ECCI (now Imerys) china clay lorries; the single-carriageway Pinnock Tunnel is now controlled by traffic lights.

There were two points of rail access to Par Harbour. One was a trailing connection (opened in 1910 and closed in 1965) from the down main line, and the other was from St Blazey depot, across the road at Par Bridge, under the Cornish main line and into the docks area. The latter is now the only route open, and a few times each week, but unscheduled and at irregular intervals, a train still makes its way down into the harbour for loading. For several decades in the diesel era this was always the work of a Class 08 shunter, but during 2007 the shunter was dispensed with by the English, Welsh & Scottish freight company

Charlestown Harbour (SX 039515) could become heavily congested and it was said that you could walk from one side of the dock to the other across the decks of ships. Except for a couple of local clay driers, for well over a century china clay and stone had to be conveyed to the harbour by road, using horse and cart formations. Payloads could vary from between 2 and 5 tons and the practice did not finally end until 1949! Here a load of china stone is loaded by hand into an early steamer. The horse on the right seems to be having his lunch! *Author's collection*

(now DB Schenker) and now main-line 125-tonne Class 66 diesel locomotives work the trains. This makes a fascinating sight on grass-covered track passing the old manual crossing gates at Par Bridge. China clay is still dried at Par Harbour 24 hours a day, seven days a week, but the docks are in a secure area and cannot be visited without appointment.

Charlestown

Whereas the port of Par was all about the Treffry family, Charlestown was the preserve of the Rashleigh family. They also had mining and china clay interests and recognised the need for an artificial harbour at West Polmear, south-east of St Austell, where hitherto ships had been simply beached and their cargo unloaded and loaded on the sand, leaving them exposed to wind, weather and tide. Charles Rashleigh (1747-1823) was the founder of Charlestown and not surprisingly the new port carried his name. He was an influential individual, being a Deputy Sheriff of Cornwall, Land Agent for the Duchy of Cornwall, Town Clerk of St Austell and the Recorder of several courts. As if to rival Treffry, he owned a tin-smelting business, had mining interests, and owned and ran a bank and two legal practices.

Prior to 1790 West Polmear had been just a tiny fishing hamlet in a cove where a few fishermen and their families scratched a living, but where increasingly ships called to service the mining industry. This arrangement was inadequate if the local mines and the

Just to the right of the yacht's mast is the sole remaining china clay loading chute. In days gone by clay would be unloaded either from a tramway that ran along the eastern side of the dock, or from wagons or trucks arriving by road. The clay was directed into the chute and down into the hold of the waiting ship. In the early days there were fishing boats using the port, but they gave way to outbound mineral ores, china clay and stone, and incoming coal and general merchandise. Nowadays it is mostly tourists who occupy the quiet harbour area, seen here in 2002. *Author*

In this wonderful July 1955 view the very last coastal sailing schooner to operate around the coasts of Britain, the *Kathleen & May*, is featured on the right. Built in 1900 by Ferguson & Baird at Connah's Quay in Flintshire, she could carry a 240-ton cargo with a crew of seven. After the Second World War she had an engine fitted. Her commercial career ended in 1960 and she is now permanently exhibited at St Katharine's Dock in London. She was a frequent visitor to Par and Charlestown, as was the coaster *Annuity* on the left. Note the splendid line-up of loading chutes. *Author's collection*

china clay industry were to be properly served, and a harbour with permanent quays was deemed necessary. Accordingly Rashleigh carved a port out of the surrounding landscape. Part of the surrounding hillside was removed and excavations were considerable because the designer, John Smeaton, an eminent engineer, wanted an inner dock that would retain its water at low tide, which meant installing lock gates at the harbour entrance. A source of top-up water was provided by a 4-mile-long leat, all the way from the Luxulyan Valley. The harbour and the surrounding buildings were constructed over a 10-year period and what emerged from this development period was an inn and the premises of a shipwright and rope-maker, a lime kiln, a pilchard cellar and later a chapel, a foundry and a tin-smelter, as well as a number of fishermen's cottages.

The port was an immediate commercial success and two regular routes to Bristol and London were established, but what was surprising was the large number of European ports served from Charlestown. At random these locations included Isigny, Nantes, Libourne, Rotterdam, Amsterdam, Bruges, Ghent, Antwerp, Bilbao, Santander, Viborg, Abo, Kotka, Riga and many, many others. In the early days copper ore and tin smelting kept the port very busy indeed; for example, in 1814 no less than 10,000 tons of copper ore was taken from the nearby Crinnis mine, and in 1824 St Austell smelting houses produced 4,137 blocks of tin. When the metalliferous mining in Cornwall collapsed, china clay broadly filled the void. It is now difficult to imagine the scene at Charlestown, but not being rail-connected (except for a wagonway from a local kiln) its entire china clay shipments arrived at the port by horse and cart. In 1850 a staggering 15,000 wagon-loads of china clay arrived and the harbour was wedged with ships. On the inbound side there were voluminous shipments of coal, timber and general merchandise. In the summer months all was well, but in the winter the local roads became deeply rutted, or 'torn to pieces' as some reports stated. The very wide approach road to the harbour was six wagons wide to accommodate the 150 clay carriers, who were mostly farmers who regarded haulage work as a profitable sideline.

One of the most interesting aspects of Charlestown's activity was the china clay loading that originated at a large clay-drying plant, a short distance from the harbour. China clay was piped down from Carglaze pit and dried at Charlestown No 1 China Clay Kiln, which was opened in Edwardian times. The clay was then transported in tippler wagons along a 2ft 4in-gauge tramway to a point above the harbour where it was discharged through special chutes into the hulls of ships, until about 1960. Latterly these were used by road transport, which discharged loads of about 20 tons per lorry into the same chutes. Today the Georgian harbour of Charlestown is a tourist magnet and host to historic sailing ships, which are regularly used in movies and on TV and are owned by the Square Sail Shipyard Ltd. There is also a Shipwreck and Heritage Centre.

Newquay

Today Newquay is one of Cornwall's main tourist centres and for more than a century this trade has been successfully nurtured. Visitors are attracted by the superb coastline, long sandy beaches and rocky coves and cliffs; also, in recent decades the town has for good reason become the 'surf capital' of England. However, all this activity has seen a tiny seaside hamlet of 489 in 1840 grow into a town with a current permanent population of well over 20,000 and a peak summer population of more than 100,000. The coming of the passenger railway made a major contribution to this growth, especially after 1892 when both the main line into Cornwall and the branch line serving the town were of the same gauge, eventually allowing through train working. Nowadays less than 10% of holidaymakers arrive in the area by rail and other than on summer weekends the local train service has been a disgrace, making the car, the coach and the aeroplane more attractive propositions. A more frequent service was introduced in December 2008.

There is evidence of Bronze Age and Iron Age activity around Newquay in the form of earthworks or 'barrows', which are 2,000-3,000-year-old burial places. The original name of the town was Towan Blistra ('place in the sand'). Documentary evidence shows that in 1439 the Bishop of Exeter was granted an indulgence for the construction, repair and maintenance of a 'new keye' for the rode of shipping, situated on the seashore near 'Tewen Blustey'. In the reign of Elizabeth I a Cornish historian wrote of a place called 'Newkaye' and thus it is reasonable to assume that today's town of Newquay has an ancient history of which it can be proud. The first time the name 'Newquay' appeared on a map was in 1758, and by the end of the 18th century the population was about 100. In the early years the inhabitants were engaged mainly in fishing; indeed, until about 1900 the area was famous for its pilchard and herring industries. A large number of fish cellars were built around the harbour and in the town. There was also a small

Newquay Harbour has one of the most interesting histories of any Cornish port. There is evidence of a quay at Newquay in the year 1439. In 1602 the town was known as 'Newkaye', where limited shelter was provided for small ships up to about 80 tons. The present harbour, with an enclosed area of about 3 acres, was established by the local squire Richard Lomax, who borrowed £10,000 for the purpose in the early 19th century; it was completed in 1838, two years after his death. In the early days fishing was the primary activity, and pilchards and herring were the target of local fishermen. In this remarkably animated scene from about 100 years ago, a record herring catch is commemorated. Note the hogsheads full of fish.
Newquay Old Cornwall Society

amount of mining and, of course, a modicum of farming activity.

Richard Lomax was the squire of Towan Blistra and he borrowed the sum of £10,000 in about 1831 to build a new harbour at Newquay with two quays enclosing some three acres of land, which would provide permanent loading/unloading facilities and provide shelter for shipping along the north coast during adverse weather. Unfortunately Lomax died in 1836 and the executors of the estate sold the entire undertaking to Joseph Thomas Treffry, who, as we have seen in the sections on Luxulyan and Par, wanted to connect Par on the south coast with Newquay on the north coast. He authorised the construction of the western part of the Treffry Tramways system, often referred to as the Newquay Tramway, and connected the large lead mine at East Wheal Rose with the harbour at Newquay. There were two structures of note, a high wooden viaduct across the Trenance Valley to the east of the town and the final descent from the streets of the town to the harbour down a 1 in 4½ incline through an 80-yard tunnel. This short section was worked by cables and the rest was reliant upon horse power. The original Act referred to the 'accommodation of passengers', but none were ever carried. Treffry had another 'grand plan' in his mind, and that was to build a massive 'Harbour of Refuge' incorporating part of the Towan Head, where the headland would be cut through and a huge granite wall would enclose 700 acres of water of sufficient depth for ships of any size. All shipping on Cornwall's notorious north coast could shelter at this refuge during gales and storms. Much work was completed but it was never finished due to Treffry's

Right: After the death of Richard Lomax, Joseph Thomas Treffry purchased the entire Newquay Harbour area and the surrounding estate. In addition to the new harbour Treffry had a grand plan for a vast 'Harbour of Refuge' on the eastern side of Towan Head, which would contain 700 acres of water and accommodate ships of every size sheltering from hostile weather. Construction started but due to Treffry's death in 1850 it was never finished and the work that had been completed eventually fell into the sea. This tiny piece of wall on the Towan Head headland above Little Fistral Beach is all that now remains, as seen in April 2007 (SX 799628). *Author*

Above: Between 1838 and 1872 there were north and south quays, but to increase operating flexibility the Cornwall Minerals Railway constructed a rail-served central pier, which was connected to the land by a wooden trestle. The Atlantic Hotel (top left) was built in 1892 and can be used in dating photographs. The sailing ship on the right has obviously brought a load of coal in from South Wales, as the four wagons in the foreground and two on the quayside are loaded with this fuel for the mines and clay kilns. *Author*

death in 1850. Now just a few dozen granite blocks lie strewn on the seashore and less than a dozen remain in situ.

In 1874 the Cornwall Minerals Railway, which had taken over all of the old tramway routes and constructed additional lines from Par to Fowey and connected Bugle with St Dennis Junction (plus branches), arrived in the town with the first locomotive-hauled freight traffic. In 1876 the company provided the first passenger trains on its new Fowey to Newquay service, via St Blazey. This service was operated by the GWR from 1877, and the GWR absorbed the CMR completely from 1896. It was not long before through holiday trains reached Newquay, and in 1905 the GWR opened another long branch line from Chacewater, via St Agnes and Perranporth. This gave direct access to Truro (and a rail route to Redruth and Penzance), albeit with a change of train. A large number of hotels were built in the late Victorian era to accommodate tourists and this trend continued in Edwardian times. After the First World War annual leave entitlement became more widespread and at least the middle classes found themselves with disposable income, a combination that resulted in the arrival of the annual summer holiday.

The iron mines on the nearby Perran Lode and the East Wheal Rose lead mine had ceased production by the mid-1880s and this affected the tramway traffic using Newquay Harbour. Once the CMR opened the line to Par, less and less china clay from the St Dennis area was dispatched from Newquay, a route that carried a twopence-per-ton surcharge. Coal was still imported as the harbour was nearer the South Wales source

NEWQUAY HARBOUR.

Above: Treffry had a grand plan to link the north and south Cornish coasts by a tramway. This would provide maximum flexibility and reduce the cost of transporting his ores and clay, and those of others (for a price), to either Newquay or Par. Although his tramways connected Par with Bugle and Newquay with St Dennis and East Wheal Rose, the scheme only came to fruition decades after Treffry's death. In this lovely old view in the days of sail, four small empty china clay wagons wait to be hauled up the incline from the harbour and back to the pits. *Author's collection*

In this delightful Victorian view half a dozen sailing ships of the era are visible and railway wagons appear on the various quays. As ships gained in size and as the mines closed, traffic dwindled at Newquay. From 1874 more clay was shipped via Par, and as a commercial port Newquay gradually slipped into oblivion.

The last inbound and outgoing loads were conveyed in the early 1920s when the original tramway through the streets of the town finally closed. Above the distant cliffs the town of Newquay is slowly growing as a holiday resort. *Newquay Old Cornwall Society*

than the southern ports. By 1900 the original tramway section of the CMR was in steep decline and, with the last commercial vessels calling at the port in 1922, the tramway, including the incline, closed and the tracks were lifted.

From Edwardian times the motor car and the motor bus had begun to make an impression, and before the Second World War the aeroplane became an option, at least for the upper classes. Although the wars retarded progress, after 1945 Newquay again boomed, but by the early 1960s mass car ownership, package holidays abroad and, in real terms, cheaper flights, had greatly reduced the public's dependence on rail travel. Indeed, for the last 30 years Newquay Airport has been growing. By 1963 the line to Chacewater (and Truro) had closed completely, and soon afterwards all goods facilities were withdrawn. The number of visitors to Newquay continued to increase but the railway was not a beneficiary. By 1987 the town received its last locomotive-hauled trains and at the end of the summer the signal box was closed and from that time only a single platform was used. The lovely old original granite station was later demolished in an appalling act of official vandalism and a piece of Newquay history was wiped off the map. The local service deteriorated, reducing to just four trains per day, and connections at Par were awful, often not held for late-running main-line trains. However, Newquay has retained the distinction of being the only Cornish branch line that still retains through holiday trains from London, the North of England and Scotland at weekends in the peak summer period.

In terms of industry and transport, the route of the old tramway through the town can still be traced in parts, the bus station being located on the alignment. The old incline tunnel was filled in years ago, but the portal at the harbour end can be identified. The old central stone jetty in the middle of the harbour, constructed by the CMR in 1872/3, is no longer connected to the land by a wooden trestle but is used by the occasional fishing boat and for lobster-pot storage. At high tide seals are often found in the harbour, and in the summer months pleasure boats are available. The harbour is best viewed from the historic Red Lion Hotel, where Treffry once dined. On the headland the lovely old Victorian Headland and Atlantic Hotels can be seen as well as the remains of Treffry's 'Harbour of Refuge'. However, the highlight is the steep ramp opposite the old lifeboat station, which was last used in 1934 (see page 106). A journey on the Newquay branch line is still worthwhile, especially if the traveller takes the time to research its history, in order to know what to look out for. For the children there is still an active fun railway at nearby Newquay Zoo and the delightful Trenance Gardens. A more frequent branch-line service commenced during December 2008.

In the same scene in 2007 the harbour is populated by a few pleasure craft and a handful of local fishing boats. The good ship *Trevose* is tied up to the central pier but the wooden trestle has long gone. Lobster-pots are the only signs of commercial activity, while in the background Newquay has grown out of all recognition. The magnificent coastline and beaches remain largely unchanged. *Author*

Agriculture

Various types of farming have been essential for survival since the beginning of time, and here nothing more than a broad overview of developments over the past couple of centuries are recorded. Until the population invasion of the West Country in recent times Cornwall in particular was never heavily populated; in the 19th and 20th centuries the population grew up around major market towns and those that were at the centre of mining activities. This growing population had to be fed, so agricultural developments went hand-in-hand with mining and other industries. These farming activities were varied, but dairy, cattle, poultry and arable farming were all practised. Much of the moorland and cliff-top grassland in Cornwall is inhospitable to anything other than sheep, but in other areas the soil and the climate are conducive to a wider range of activities.

There is little doubt that over the years technological innovation has had an enormous impact, whether it be in the world of machinery, power sources or fertilisers. Overall Cornish farms have tended to be smaller than in the rest of the UK. For example, the average UK farm is 73 hectares, whereas in Cornwall the average is 43 hectares, with nearly half being less than 20 hectares. The number of people employed

Agriculture and farming were practised by the Celts in Cornwall back in the Iron Age, and the 'industry' as such has a long tradition. From a period of simple self-sufficiency, farming has now grown into a modern business, which in recent years has had more than its share of problems. During the past century technology, especially in respect of farm machinery, has had an enormous impact in reducing manual labour. In this delightful post-Second World War scene a farmer outside Restormel Manor is taking delivery of his new Ferguson tractor, which will be serviced by Par Engineering & Motor Works Ltd, telephone 'Par 49'! *Cornish Studies Library*

Prior to 1600 Cornish sheep produced poor-quality wool, but by selective breeding over the centuries this is no longer the case. When compared to many other English counties Cornwall does not have extensive arable land, so sheep have helped fill a void. In recent years more farms have, for economic reasons, abandoned dairy farming and converted to cattle and sheep. Here a flock moves around the boundary of Restormel Castle in 1995. *Author*

in the industry has plummeted. In 1861 15,291 were employed on the land, but by 1931, despite a greatly increased population, this had fallen to 9,156. In real terms this number has fallen again, although the emergence of large garden and horticulture centres has corrupted modern statistics. About two-thirds of Cornwall's farms are owner-occupied and the other third are rented. Overall, all types of farming have become less important in manpower terms, accounting for only about 1 in 25 jobs, whereas tourism and associated activities account for 1 in 4 of Cornwall's employed population, albeit with seasonal elements. Politics and legislation have a great deal to do with the finances and farming finances in particular. *The Times* newspaper pointed out in 2001 that Cornwall was getting poorer compared with the rest of the UK, and claimed that the reason was that out of a Gross Domestic Product of £3.6 billion HM Treasury extracted £1.95 billion in taxation, giving back only £1.65 billion by way of grants and refunds. Per capita Cornwall's GDP was a mere 62% of the national average and the county was one of only four areas in the UK that qualified for poverty-related grants. It was recognised that there were significant fluctuations in Cornwall's wealth from area to area, but overall the picture was not rosy. Since that report Cornwall's population has increased to well over 500,000 and property prices in the South West have increased more than anywhere else in the UK, on a percentage gain basis.

During the past 20 years European legislation and the enormous power of the major food retailers have influenced farming in Cornwall and the rest of the UK. Dairy herds, for example, have dwindled by more than 20% and pig-farming is down by 8%. On the up side, beef farming has increased by nearly 60% and sheep by just 2%. Due to a complex farm subsidy structure there has been a move away from cereal crops, especially spring and winter barley because margins have been reduced, which has forced farmers into higher-margin crops. However alien to Cornwall these crops might be, favourable subsidies have resulted in a vast increase in oilseed rape, linseed and maize. Despite changes in trends and subsidies, the overall farming income has, in real terms, fallen significantly, and in order to survive farmers have had little choice but to diversify. In fact, 65% of all farms now operate a farm processing and sales system, with some direct interaction with local retailers or the general public. Also, members of the farming family have been economically forced into 'off-farm employment', where either full- or

During the last couple of decades there has been a gradual move from rented farms to wholly-owned farms. There have also been large increases in horticultural activity on farms and, due to various subsidies, crops of sugar beet, field beans, dry peas, oilseed rape and maize have increased. Because of external pricing pressures the number of dairy herds has been decimated during the past 20 years, and pig and poultry-farming have also decreased. Here we see some ploughing activity at Lower Dowgas Farm, west of St Austell, in 1995. *Author*

part-time employment has to be taken away from the home farm, especially on small units where diversification may not be possible.

Over the years the introduction of farm machinery has had an enormous impact on farm efficiency, productivity and the labour force. Some modern machinery performs the task of scores of men, and the leasing of large machines, such as combine harvesters, helps avoid seasonal peaks and troughs in manpower and the requirement for major capital investment on a disproportionate scale. In the 19th century steam engines and water-powered machinery helped with the drudgery of many manual activities and the humble farm tractor was a revelation in the amount of work of every description that could be undertaken in the field. Machines were designed and built to perform the majority of tasks on the farm and the writer always remembers the first visit to Dairyland in Cornwall during the 1970s where a totally automated milking process for dozens of cows, who revolved on a turntable, made a fascinating sight for the visiting holiday-makers.

Further changes over the centuries have involved the various yields that have been secured per acre. In the days of old Cornish farmers relied on sand, lime and even seaweed to improve the quality of their soil, but for many decades ever-improving fertilisers have, at a price, become generally available. In fact, until about 1990 a special weekly fertiliser train from Ince & Elton in Cheshire delivered the commodity to Truro for onward distribution. Finally the large range of diverse crops that are grown in Cornwall must not be forgotten. In past decades the west of Cornwall became famous for its broccoli and in the season whole trainloads of the vegetable would be conveyed to the markets in London. For example, in a single day during 1896 some 174 wagons of broccoli were dispatched from four west Cornwall stations, and 40 years later, in 1936, the season's tally amounted to 30,000 tons of the stuff!

Flowers

I t is said that the far South West of the UK mainland is the best place in the world to grow certain types of flower, and the climate enables daffodils, narcissi, anemones and violets to bloom before the normal season starts. The origins of the flower industry in Cornwall date back to about 1870 when consignments started to be sent to London. There have always been two aspects to the industry: the supply of pre-season and early-season flowers, and the sale of bulbs. Flowers were a higher priority in the Isles of Scilly compared with the mainland, and their small farms, little walled fields, salty winds and limited water availability particularly suited tazetta narcissi. By 1886 flower shows and local competitions were being held in St Mary's on the Scilly Isles. On the island of St Agnes the primary occupation was flower-growing.

The business really boomed, and in 1898 the L&SWR provided competition to the GWR for a short period by shipping flowers from the Scilly Isles to its railhead at Plymouth, thereby denting the GWR's income from the traffic. In 1910 the GWR carried 450 tons of flowers to London, and by 1936 this figure had leapt to 2,432 tons! Bulbs would be planted in July and August before the ground became too wet; they could not be planted too closely otherwise the flowers would be smaller and of inferior quality. Fertiliser high in potash was used to promote growth. From time to time pests such as eel worms and narcissus fly caused disruption to the business, but cures were found. Some daffodils would be ready before the year end, giving Cornwall a huge lead in a marketplace that was becoming increasingly competitive from foreign sources. The whole process was labour-intensive until about the 1950s when mechanisation made its presence felt. However, by this time the flowers-by-rail traffic was in decline and eventually the 'perishables' trade on British Railways petered out. By the 1970s the motor lorry became the preferred mode of transport for this still buoyant industry.

One industry that benefited hugely from the coming of the railway was flower-growing. Particularly in the Scilly Isles but also around Mount's Bay on the mainland, the climate enabled what would normally be regarded as out-of-season flowers to be grown, picked and rushed to major cities by train. In 1910 no less than 450 tons of flowers were dispatched to London during the year. This view shows a flower farm on the Isles of Scilly, where daffodils and narcissi were grown in huge numbers. *Author's collection*

Lime kilns

The process of burning limestone in a kiln to produce lime mortar for use as a bonding agent in the construction of stone buildings and as a lime plaster for covering walls and ceilings can be traced back more than 4,000 years. Apparently there is a surviving detailed account of the lime-burning process that dates back to Roman times. There are various types of limestone and all are forms of calcium carbonate. If calcium carbonate, clay and sand are mixed, a substance called 'marl' is formed, and more than 2,000 years ago it was discovered that the use of marl in soil improved its fertility. The soil in much of Cornwall is acidic, and the application of shell-based sands also helped with fertility and had been used for some time. There is little limestone in Cornwall, so when lime kilns started to be built in some numbers, between 1690 and 1820, limestone had to be imported from Devon for south coast sites and from South Wales for lime kilns on the north coast.

The population of Cornwall was increasing and as a result farming became a little more intensive. To improve the soil lime kilns started to be built along the coastline of Cornwall at locations where the limestone could be landed from ships. This was usually in ports and harbours or along tidal creeks and estuaries. From the kilns lime, or more correctly quicklime, would be carted to the farms for application. The quicklime broke down organic matter, which released nitrogen for reuse as a plant food. It also improved aeration of the soil, which helped with drainage. Above all it neutralised acidic soils and provided plant food, leading to healthy crops.

To provide a heat source for burning the limestone in a kiln, lime-burners used whatever fuel was to hand or easily available, such as wood, coal, turf, peat and culm. There were several different types of lime kiln, but most of those found in Cornwall were vertical shaft kilns. To the layman these large stone structures are most easily identified by their high round arches, which invite the viewer into the structure but seemingly go nowhere. These kilns are typically 20 feet square and 15 feet high with a circular central shaft, known as the 'pot'. At the base of the shaft was a draw-

The purpose of lime kilns was to convert limestone into lime for agricultural purposes, normally to improve the soil. Lime was also used in the building industry as a bonding agent in mortar and plaster, and for covering walls and ceilings. There was little limestone in Cornwall and nearly all of the material had to be imported; lime kilns on the south coast were fed from Devon and those on the north coast from South Wales. These fine kilns are located at Moorswater near the old Liskeard & Looe Canal basin (SX 236641). *Author*

Lime kilns can come in any configuration, but normally there are between one and three kilns in any single location. This magnificent trio of arches at Cotehele Quay (SX 423680), below Cotehele House, provides access to two pots. Nearby are further lime kilns, and the whole site was a form of distribution point for the surrounding area. There are no fewer than 18 lime kiln sites on the Cornish side of the River Tamar between Saltash and Gunnislake; the last to operate was in 1916. *Author*

hole through which burnt lime could be removed. Sometimes a kiln would have two or more 'pots' and the precise internal configuration could vary from kiln to kiln. In some, fuel and stone were loaded in alternate layers while in others the heat source was introduced through the side of the kiln from a separate firebox. It was the lime-burner's job to ensure that the fire received the correct draught to burn at the right temperature and to handle the output.

The remains of lime kilns can be found throughout Cornwall and more than 200 separate sites have been identified. About 80% are located on the south coast, the other 20% being along the north coast, an area where shelly sand was available, which was often used for the same purpose as quicklime, both containing calcium carbonate. These old lime kilns are in varying states of either decay or preservation, but they are a fascinating part of Cornwall's industrial past and are certainly worth seeking out.

Brewing

There can be few Cornish industries where, over a period of 200 years, there has been such volatility in terms of the number of active breweries, their owners, their retail outlets, their products and the licensees purveying the product. In the old days local and coaching inns were the main focal point for the purchase and consumption of alcohol; some of today's survivors date back to medieval times and are well worth discovering. In the late 18th and early 19th centuries brewing was undertaken on a small scale by today's standards with local brewhouses, often linked with a public house, brewing their own beer for local consumption. Many country houses brewed their own strong barley wines and it was often the butler who was 'head brewer' for the gentry. In the commercial brewhouses the beer tended to be stored for months in unlined wooden vessels known as tuns. It would pick up some lactic sourness from the content of the wood and be dubbed 'stale' by drinkers, resulting in the expression 'old ale'. Later in the 19th century the more enterprising local brewers recognised the demands of the growing population and built additional pubs, which became part of the brewers' estates. They also moved away from vatted beers and developed 'running beers' that could be served after just a few days' storage in pub cellars. New technologies allowed brewers to use a variety of malts, hops and other natural ingredients to produce pale ale and bitters as well as mild beer, in varying strengths.

By about 1850 there were 12 Cornish breweries of substance. The largest were in Albaston, Liskeard, St Austell, Falmouth, Penryn, Redruth and Hayle. Worthy of special mention was the Redruth brewery owned by Magor Davey & Co, which was established in 1742. Even in those early days there were amalgamations and takeovers, and the Redruth company expanded by taking over, for example, W. & E. C. Carne & Co of Falmouth, before itself being taken over by Devenish & Co of Weymouth in the 1930s. The brewery closed in 2004 and its steam engine was said to be the last to be genuinely used in a commercial application in the whole of Cornwall. A great survivor in Cornwall is the St Austell Brewery Co Ltd, founded by Walter Hicks in 1851. By 1867 he had built a steam brewery in the town and by 1893/4 a completely new and stylish brewery was constructed, which is still in operation today (SX 017528) offering brewery tours for the general public.

In more recent years there have been significant changes on the

One of the oldest industries in Cornwall, and elsewhere for that matter, is brewing. Over the centuries minor breweries have come and gone and corporate takeovers have had a profound effect. There were 12 Cornish breweries circa 1850 and this number had increased to 20 by 1897. In 2006 there were 16 independent brewers in Cornwall, with St Austell, Sharp's and Skinner's seemingly in the lead with a bunch of micro-breweries snapping at their heels. This ancient view shows the 'Old Inn' at St Ives, where William Hollow was the licensee. *Author's collection*

national brewing scene. For those who appreciate the taste of local beers the seemingly perpetual takeover of local, regional and family-owned breweries by monster 'national' breweries has been a retrograde step. Their obsession with producing gassy keg beer and cold tasteless lagers filled with chemicals, combined with aggressive marketing and advertising campaigns, has put smaller firms at risk and many hundreds have closed their doors forever. However, the Campaign for Real Ale (CAMRA) co-ordinated customer resistance to this trend and there is no doubt that its influence has helped perpetuate the survival of traditional British beer. In more recent times so called 'micro-breweries' have sprung up all over the country, including Cornwall, but many have found the going tough because of the stranglehold that the national brewers and certain 'pub chains' have on retail outlets. Nationally, about 20 micro-breweries are established each year and the same number fail. However, in 2004 the Government introduced Progressive Beer Duty, whereby micros and small regional breweries with an output of less than 30,000 barrels of beer per year pay less duty.

There are now about 500 micro- and 35 family-owned breweries in operation in the UK. In Cornwall in 2007 St Austell Brewery, Sharp's Brewery at Rock and Skinner's Brewery at Truro were all producing excellent beers. Cornish micro-brewers included Ales of Scilly at St Mary's, Atlantic at Treisaac, Blackawton at Saltash, Blue Anchor at Helston, Coastal at Redruth, Doghouse at Scorrier, Driftwood at Trevaunance Cove (St Agnes), Keltek at Lostwithiel, Lizard at St Keverne, Organic at Curry Cross Lanes, and Wooden Hand at Grampound Road. These Cornish beers can be found throughout the county's pubs, whether they be free houses in delightful rural settings or tied pubs in busy towns, and all are well worth trying.

Above: In some respects pubs are as important as the breweries, and in Cornwall there are some truly ancient establishments. Located in the heart of china clay country at Carthew is the Sawles Arms, a tied St Austell house. One wonders how many pints have been drunk and how many pasties have been consumed over the decades by the local workforce. Certainly there was a medicinal need for all of that china clay dust to be washed through the system! The tail end of the old Goonbarrow branch line was located just to the right of the pub, at SX 005563. *Author*

Below: A wonderful free house and one-time winner of CAMRA's pub of the year is The Blisland Inn, located in the village of the same name between the River Camel and Bodmin Moor. The pub serves a wide range of real ales, and the old granite building has been the centre of village life for years. The local church was one of Sir John Betjeman's favourites and it too has its share of visitors. One problem with retaining village pubs in Cornwall is their potential value as dwelling houses, resulting in many closures and 'change of use' orders in recent years. *Author*

Fishing

Traditionally, and certainly before the development of the china clay industry, fishing was described as one of the largest three industries in Cornwall, the others being mining and farming. This was hardly surprising when much of the county is located within a dozen miles of either the north or south coast. In the early days fish was an important part of the staple Cornish diet and every port and cove was involved in the fishing industry, using any vessel that was capable of floating. However, over the years the industry has suffered from more and more control, leaving only four ports with what could be called large-scale activity: these are (with their 1997 annual catch values in millions) Newlyn (£23.4), Falmouth (£3.7m), Looe (£3.1) and Padstow (£2.5).

Life as a fisherman has always been harsh, but one of contrast, to a considerable extent predicated by the weather and the seasons. Especially before modern communications and sophisticated meteorology evolved it was easy for even an experienced fisherman to be caught in a storm and with only sail power available the risk to the boat and to life itself was high. Many boats worked up to 50 miles from the shore and running for shelter could take many hours. There are countless stories of ships being smashed to pieces on reefs and rocks with a commensurately high casualty rate. As a small example, in 1817 a terrible storm saw 30 of Polperro's 45 fishing boats destroyed, and again in 1824 a further 19 boats were destroyed. The coastguard, lighthouses and lifeboat services were established and in recent decades they have been supplemented by air/sea rescue activities involving aircraft. Historically whole families were involved in the fishing industry, with the men manning the boats and preparing the ship and equipment and the women salting, pressing, bulking and cleaning the fish. The seasons were also significant because certain types of fish were plentiful only for a few months of the year, especially the important pilchard industry.

Pilchards are smaller than mackerels but larger than sardines. They always appeared off the Cornish coast in large shoals and the fishing fleets employed spotters or 'huers' to locate them by observing gulls and disturbance in the water. Ports such as Newquay relied on

In the eyes of many Cornish fishermen their industry has been under attack for several decades as they face reductions in quotas and a barrage of European legislation. They also regularly observe foreign vessels making super-catches off Cornish shores without knowing whether they are complying with the 'rules'. A port that still sees fishing activities, albeit on a hugely reduced scale from its halcyon days, is Padstow. Showing her registration PW 240 and the Cornish flag of St Pirran on her bow, the good ship *Diligence* is about to berth at Padstow with the day's catch in September 2006. *Author*

pilchard fishing and, to a lesser extent, herring fishing for their very existence. The pilchards were encircled and caught in nets by the seining process. They were then stored in cellars, large enough to contain 500 hogsheads (straight-sided barrels), each containing about 3,000 pilchards. The fish were prepared with salt then pressed so that the oil drained out as a by-product and was sold. Much of the catch was exported to Italy and Spain and other Mediterranean countries. The pilchards stopped visiting the north Cornwall coast in about 1893 and all of Newquay's fish cellars closed within a decade or so. Fishing for herring continued until the First World War, but nowadays only shellfish are landed.

Just about every Cornish harbour and port has had some involvement in the fishing industry over the years, an inevitable situation in a county that is almost surrounded by the ocean. However, there has been a massive downturn in the industry, and today many minor Cornish ports cater only for the occasional social yachtsman. This postcard, dating back to 5 September 1910, shows a sight that is but a memory, the Newquay fishing 'fleet'. Once a centre for large-scale pilchard and herring fishing, only the occasional crustacean is now landed. *Author's collection*

The Cornish fishermen are a close-knit community. They consider that they have been sold short by progressive UK governments as reduced quotas have been imposed and vigorous action has not been taken in defending coastal waters from European poachers. When the Canadian Navy intercepted and impounded a Portuguese fishing boat off Newfoundland for illegal activities every port in Cornwall and most fishing vessels flew the Canadian flag for some time, emphasising the perceived impotence of UK fishery protection activities. Reduced landing quotas, increased red tape and restricted income have unfortunately led to boat decommissioning and scrapping.

Newlyn

Newlyn is the fishing capital of Cornwall, and is the largest fishing port in England. A visit to the harbour and time spent watching the frenetic activity just after the fishing fleet has landed reveals a remarkable phenomenon. The sheds are packed with boxes of fish packed in ice and fishermen and workers dressed in yellow oilskins are everywhere. There are forklift trucks, small tractors or 'tugs' and refrigerated lorries waiting to be loaded. There is the fishing mission, the fish market, harbour offices, lifeboat station (where the Penlee lifeboat is now moored), pontoons for private yachts and the various piers. The only worrying aspect is the impression given that there are significantly more fishing boats tied up than in active service. The largest operator is W. Stevenson & Sons with 35 boats, 150 seafaring fishermen and 90 shore staff; the company's trawlers are the largest vessels in port. Many of the other trawlers and fishing boats are owned by their skippers. Generally boats under 30 feet in length fish only in inshore waters.

Top: The epicentre of the Cornish fishing industry is Newlyn, a couple of miles south-west of Penzance. Documents from 1435 refer to a quay that accommodated 40 boats, so the history of fishing at this location is well established! This early Edwardian real photographic view shows the old and original quay at Newlyn, now dwarfed by later developments. A few small sailing boats shelter behind the granite wall on what seems to be a calm day. *Author's collection*

Right: This is almost the same scene in March 2007. The railings, the steps and the outer wall are all the same but a small building has been erected on the quay, a vast number of fishing boats are berthed in the harbour, and the town of Newlyn in the background seems to have grown somewhat. In 1997 the annual value of the fish landed at Newlyn was £23.4 million. *Author*

All operators are under pressure and there have been recent allegations of exceeding fishing quotas that have resulted in court proceedings being instituted. Other than simply making a living from fishing, there are a number of pressures on the fishing fleet, including the sheer nonsense of current regulations. Officials do not seem to realise that in trying to catch one type of fish it is inevitable that other species are caught. One recent heartbreaking story involved a Newlyn skipper having to dump 1,000 dead cod into the sea, rather than illegally land his catch and exceed the quota. The fleet at Newlyn has to cope daily with this lunacy, which stems from the Common Fisheries Policy.

The scores of fishing boats at Newlyn land more than 80 different species of fish. The majority are exported and for centuries the countries around the Mediterranean have been the primary recipients. This traffic results in foreign vessels entering the port. There are many different types of fishing boat, such as trawlers, netters and crabbers, each equipped to catch and land a specific type of fish. As quotas change fishermen have to be flexible in changing their target catch. Generally small trawlers of about 40 feet in length will have a crew of two or three, but this complement triples on the larger vessels. Having caught the fish, deep-sea fishermen must gut, clean and box the catch on the return journey to harbour. In the past thousands of tons of fish per annum were sent from Penzance to Billingsgate Market in London, where the population could eat fish

36 hours after it had been caught. In 1879 it cost £4 per ton to send fish from Penzance to London, and on the heaviest single day a staggering 200 tons of fish were conveyed – big business indeed. During peak periods special trains were arranged. The GWR was accused of abusing its monopoly and of profiteering by charging more than six times the tariff for fish compared to general goods. Relationships between the railway and the owners of the fisheries became very strained indeed. In 1895 the combined catches of Newlyn and Penzance were 6,720 tons, worth nearly £100,000.

Slowly but surely sail gave way to steam, and later diesel engines kept the fleet moving, a much safer and more reliable form of propulsion, except for those romantically inclined! By the turn of the 20th century the fishing industry at Newlyn was booming and it now seems strange to relate that within 50 years fish would no longer be conveyed by rail.

Newlyn is a very old harbour and even its 'recent' history dates back to 1435, when a harbour wall affording protection for 40 boats was built. This harbour wall survives at old Newlyn, the lower modern 40-acre harbour having been built on reclaimed land in 1885-8. The town was largely destroyed during a Spanish raid in 1595. One metal plaque in the town suggests that the *Mayflower* docked at Newlyn Old Quay on 16 August 1620 for water and supplies before its historic crossing of the Atlantic Ocean, the water supply at Plymouth being contaminated with cholera. Another plaque celebrates the departure of the fishing lugger *Mystery*, which left Newlyn on 18 November 1854 bound for Australia, safely arriving four months later on 14 March 1855.

The town rises steeply from the harbour and is steeped in history. Over the years its growth has been remarkable. From a population of 735 in 1801 it had grown to a whopping 21,168 by 2001, and in residential terms has been connected to Penzance for years. There are even traffic jams during peak periods. Its streets are worth exploring and it is hardly surprising that the many public houses in the area are festooned with nautical paintings, photographs and maritime bric-a-brac. There is an annual Newlyn Fish Festival, which attracts large crowds.

This ancient view from the reign of Queen Victoria shows the Newlyn fleet comprising mostly sailing ships, with just one steamer at the dockside. There are just a handful of houses at Newlyn and the tourist industry has yet to become established. Today just over 50% of the fish caught commercially in the UK is landed in the South West, although that figure includes ports in Devon and Dorset. *Author's collection*

Newlyn Pilchard Works (SW 462291) can be visited and the traditional way of pressing and curing pilchards can be observed. In October 2007 HRH The Princess Royal unveiled a memorial to all Cornish and Isles of Scilly fishermen lost at sea. The life-size bronze statue is mounted on three large granite slabs dredged from Newlyn Harbour.

An interesting curio at Newlyn was the Penlee Quarry railway. Work started at Penlee Quarry just after 1890 and by about 1900 a 2-foot-gauge railway line had been opened to convey the stone to a pier at Newlyn, where the output was shipped. The quarried stone was transported by conveyor belts to crushers and loading hoppers adjacent to the railway. The line ran for about three-quarters of a mile with sidings, storage areas and an engine shed. In the past the quarry had been owned by Roads Reconstruction Ltd and later by ARC (Southwestern) Ltd. Originally a steam locomotive was used for traction but from the early 1950s diesels were in charge. Rail traffic ceased from 31 July 1972 and the quarry closed completely in the 1980s.

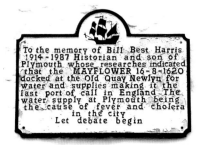

Above: Newlyn is proud of its history and a number of signs and items of memorabilia are scattered about the area. This interesting sign is displayed on a building just above the Old Quay, but in 1620 there were no cameras available to prove the point! *Author*

Above: Inevitably there have been a number of interesting sailings from Newlyn over the years and this must have been one of them. It is hard to imagine spending four months cooped up on a small fishing lugger, fighting heavy seas, eating heavily salted food and drinking stagnant water. *Author*

There was a quaint narrow-gauge railway in the Newlyn area that ran from the South Pier to Penlee Quarry, which produced baked dolerite (blue elvan) stone. The quarry opened in 1890 and a 2-foot-gauge railway was in operation by 1900. Rail traffic ceased in 1972 and conveyor belts took over, then the quarry closed completely in the 1980s. Its last owners were ARC (Southwestern) Ltd. Here *Penlee* 0-4-0T heads a train of tipplers to the quarry. Note the bowler hat! *M. Dart collection*

Canals

Liskeard and Looe Union Canal

In the late 18th century the town of Liskeard was well established. It was linked by a turnpike road to Torpoint in the 1770s, thus improving transportation for the population generally and greatly facilitating the movement of goods. However, it was not until the end of the century that the first wagons started to appear. Most of Liskeard's imported and exported goods were taken to and from the quay at St Germans. As mentioned in other chapters the Cornish soil here was acidic and a series of lime kilns had been constructed along the East Looe river valley between the port of Looe and Liskeard. The limestone was conveyed by packhorses and, after burning, the quicklime needed to be distributed in the fields at a rate of 4 to 5 tons per acre. To accommodate this traffic and other merchandise a survey was conducted in 1777 to test the feasibility of building a canal between the two centres. An interesting piece of social history appears in the specification, when the surveyor suggests that two inclined planes could

Above: The undulating Cornish terrain was not, in general terms, conducive to canal building, but they were nevertheless considered to be the solution to some serious transportation problems in the late 18th and early 19th centuries. Proposals for new canals and subsequent surveys greatly exceeded the number actually built and today their remains are few and far between. A successful canal, at least until the railway arrived, was the 6-mile-long Liskeard & Looe Union Canal, which opened between Moorswater basin near Liskeard to Terras Bridge, near Looe, in 1828. This view shows the tidal lock at Terras Bridge just after closure of the lower part of the canal in 1910. *Royal Institute of Cornwall*

Above: This is the same view at Terras Bridge almost a century later, in September 2007. The old lock is occupied by a decaying boat but the position of the canal and the lock gates can still be identified. The branch line survived and a Class 153 diesel unit can be seen scuttling by on its way to Liskeard. The railway opened in 1860 and shortly afterwards the canal closed beyond Sandplace. This interesting and scenic location can be found at SW 249557. *Author*

At certain points in the valley of the East Looe River the railway, the old canal, the river and the road all run parallel. The valley is heavily overgrown but traces of the old canal can still be found, especially near road overbridges. With the archway of the abandoned canal on the right, single diesel unit No 55000 arrives at St Keyne station with the 16.54 Liskeard to Looe service on 2 April 1990. Note the GWR station seat. *Author*

be powered by water-wheels or by 'convicts in walking wheels'! Broadly following the contours of the countryside, the meandering canal would have been 15 miles long to cover less than half that distance 'as the crow flies'.

Nothing transpired following the original survey and a further scheme was considered after a survey in 1795. This proposal did not follow the contours and as a result the route was shorter but incorporated a large number of locks. Inactivity turned to local frustration and in 1823 a public meeting was called to consider the improvement of communication between Liskeard and Looe by either 'a Turnpike Road, a Rail Road, or a Canal'. Although the meeting was positive and a considerable number of costed permutations were considered, such deliberations did not manifest themselves into actual construction work. However, a Bill for a canal was passed by both Houses and received the Royal Assent in June 1825. The capital required was £13,000 and the canal was to be completed within five years. By this time the mines and quarries around Caradon Hill were beginning to grow, so the canal would not only handle incoming limestone, coal and timber but also outgoing ore and stone. The water supply was to come from the East Looe River and the Crylla stream, with the waters of the infant River Fowey making a minor seasonal contribution.

The canal was to be 26 feet wide at the surface, 14 feet wide at the bottom and 4 feet deep. The canal boats were to have a capacity of 20 tons. By June 1826 several of the 24 locks had been built and, indeed, a demonstration of their ability to function was organised. However, there were financial problems in that not all of the allotted shares had been taken up and paid for. Part of the canal opened in August 1827 and a new simplified list of toll rates was produced. Burnt lime was 3d (3 old pence) per ton mile, ores and metals 4d, grain, flour, potatoes, salt, timber, bricks and the like 6d and most other goods, including livestock, 8d. At this time the main imports were limestone, sand, coal and culm. The canal was in full use by 1828, although various works still had to be completed.

Although the cost of coal and lime in the Liskeard area decreased as a result of the opening of the canal, the owners of lime kilns near Sandplace were aggrieved that their kilns were being under-used or not used at all, with commensurate financial losses. Lime kilns had been built around the basin at Moorswater, saving the farmers several miles in cartage, and small tramways were used to connect the basin quays to the lime kilns. The canal made a small profit of a few hundred pounds each year, but with some dodgy accounting and a lack of supervision over repairs its operations were marginal. Fortunately traffic began to increase as there was further mining activity in the hills north of Liskeard, and volumes were so high by 1846 that a railway line was completed from the Cheesewring, via South Caradon (see the earlier section on Quarries) to Moorswater. In the following years the canal company's profits increased. These were to be the halcyon days of the L&LUC. In 1849 the canal conveyed 21,713 tons, including 7,546 tons of copper and 6,175 tons of coal. By 1859 this had increased by a staggering 122% with the total conveyed amounting to a colossal 48,193 tons (including 17,361 tons of copper ore and 15,712 tons of coal, the carriage of limestone having substantially decreased). Annual profits exceeded £2,000. With only 13 boats available, carrying 16 tons each (less than the original barges) and with eight hours being required for the 7-mile journey from Moorswater to Looe Harbour, the canal was working to capacity.

To resolve the problem a feasibility and costing study was authorised in 1857 to consider the provision of a railway line. This could be provided for a modest £11,000 and a Bill for its construction received Royal Assent in May 1858. This was very timely as the proposers were well aware that the Cornwall Railway was building the main line through Cornwall and, once open, much of their traffic could be lost. Also the building of the railway would allow through running from the mines and quarries to the port at Looe, avoiding any form of intermediate transhipment. Work on the line to Looe started in 1859. As a result of financial problems concerning working capital, an arrangement was made for the Liskeard & Caradon Railway to buy the wagons and for the Liskeard & Looe Union Canal company to hire the locomotive! There was a grand opening on 27 December 1860 when the locomotive and 12 open goods trucks, fitted out for the occasion, carried the Directors, local dignitaries, 'several gentlemen', a band, many of the members and a host of other persons. The train left Moorswater at 10.00am, arriving at Looe a few minutes after 11. There were joyous scenes at Looe and according to reports the streets were gaily decorated with evergreen arches. A public dinner followed. However, it would be a further 19 years before passengers would be carried over the line. Following the opening of the railway traffic boomed. Late in 1862 it was reported that trade at Looe harbour had increased by 300% in ten years! However, by 1863 ores from the mines had peaked and in terms of mineral traffic the railway payloads declined.

Looking along the alignment of the Liskeard & Looe Union Canal from Coombe Junction towards Moorswater Viaduct on 3 February 1988, we see Class 37 No 37672 creeping along the single-track freight-only line from Moorswater clay driers with a rake of loaded clay hood wagons bound for Fowey. This traffic ceased in 1997 and the line was closed, only to be reopened for infrequent cement traffic. *Author*

It was hardly surprising in the circumstances that the condition of the canal declined rapidly. By 1867 the residents of Duloe (a village between Moorswater and Looe, located slightly away from the canal/railway) said that the canal was useless. By this time it seems unlikely that there was any canal traffic beyond Sandplace, and that was purely of an agricultural nature. In later years the canal became silted up and choked by weeds, its banks gradually crumbled away and only very small boats capable of carrying just over a ton of sand or seaweed belonging to the tenants of the various estates were using the

Above: The comparison between this and the following photograph is approaching the unbelievable. On 31 August 1954 three trains are visible: 2-6-2T Prairie tank No 4526 has just run round the Looe goods train at Coombe Junction, while a sister locomotive waits for the road in the background, having just come up from Moorswater; in the meantime a down express with a GWR/WR 4-6-0 in charge can be seen crossing Moorswater Viaduct, nearly 150 feet above the valley floor. The Lamellion Wool Combing Mill on the right has already been featured. *R. C. Riley/Transport Treasury*

Right: With the footpath and the fencing on the right being common to both photographs, it is almost impossible to accept that this is almost the same view but exactly 50 years later, in September 2004. Single-car unit No 153318 is about to leave the Coombe Junction platform with a train from Liskeard to Looe. Unchecked foliage has obliterated the view of the small road overbridge and Moorswater Viaduct, resulting in a very sylvan image. The course of the old canal was immediately to the right of the fence. *Author*

lower part. After the GWR took over in 1909 the canal finally died, but at the northern Moorswater end it had fallen out of use many decades before.

Today there are still traces of the old Liskeard & Looe Union Canal, mainly in the form of the overbridges carrying roads across the river, the old canal and the Looe branch railway line. The best open view is at Terras Pill lock, about a mile up the river from Looe (see the photographs on page 85).

Bude Canal

Due to the rugged Cornish terrain and limited water supply the option of using canals for the effective transportation of goods in large volumes was limited. Nevertheless a number of canal proposals were surveyed and costed. A few came to fruition, such as the St Columb Canal, constructed from 1773 but closed by 1781, the Liskeard & Looe Union Canal, first surveyed in 1777 and eventually built (albeit via a different route from the original plan) in 1827, and the Par Canal, to Ponts Mill and in operation from 1833. Others remained just the proposers' dreams, including North Downs to Portreath (1780), Hayle and Gweek (1796), Wadebridge to Dunmere (1797), Gwennap Mines to Restronguet Creek, near Devoran (1808), and Padstow to Fowey (1825).

Canal Locks, Bude

Above: The Bude Canal was the brainchild of John Edyvean, a Cornishman who had been a pioneer in the design and construction of the St Columb Canal. The latter was in fact two canals running inland from Mawgan Porth and St Columb Porth; these tub-boat canals were open only for a short time in the 1770s. Edyvean's dream was to connect Bude with Calstock on the River Tamar, and an Act to build the canal received Royal Assent in 1774, but lapsed without a canal being built. It was eventually opened in stages from 1823. Here we see the large canal basin and sea lock at Bude in about 1905. Note the sand tramway and the tipping wagon in the foreground. *M. Dart collection*

The total length of the canal was 35½ miles, at a cost of £120,000, a fortune in those far-off days. Other than for the first couple of miles, small tub boats were used. As roads improved, the railway network spread and the use of sand diminished, so canal traffic declined. Parts were abandoned as early as 1891, and within a decade operations had ceased. Making a refreshing change in 'before and after' comparisons, this 2001 view shows that little has changed at Bude except for a few more buildings and the absence of trading vessels. Even the sand tramway tracks have survived. Note the huge lock gates by the white fencing. *Author*

As already mentioned, one of the requirements of Cornish agriculture was a neutralising agent for the mostly acid soil. In north Cornwall this usually comprised shell-based sea sand but also quicklime, produced from limestone by heating it to a high temperature in kilns. Seaweed was also used, although only in comparatively small volumes. Lime was used more on the south coast, whereas sand was the most commonly used fertiliser in the north. There were ample supplies of shell-based sea sand full of calcium carbonate along the north coast and this could be easily extracted. However, transporting the heavy substance miles inland, into the heart of the agricultural communities, was a difficult task.

The cure for the problem was the brainchild of John Edyvean, who had been involved in the conception and building of the St Columb Canal, mentioned above. His concept was to connect Bude with the River Tamar, near Calstock, thereby penetrating farming country but also linking the Bristol and English Channels. An Act to build such a canal was given Royal Assent in May 1774. The event was significant only by its subsequent inactivity, and after a decade the Act lapsed. It was a full 30 years before the subject re-emerged, and in 1817 James Green, an engineer, and Thomas Sheaton, a surveyor, concluded that a canal was possible, but because of steeply rising land and a poor water supply, inclined planes should be used to gain elevation.

At the sea or Bude end of the canal there would be a basin, which, from 1835, was capable of taking vessels of up to 300 tons, with huge lock gates to protect the canal from rough seas but also to retain, discharge and collect water depending on the state of the tide. A protective breakwater was also proposed. Beyond the basin the canal would be narrower and shallow tub boats fitted with wheels for use on the inclined planes would be used

Postally used in 1913, this view shows Efford Cottage at Bude and a pair of trading vessels that have either used or are waiting to use the sea lock. The original lock was destroyed by a storm and in 1835 it was rebuilt and enlarged to 116ft by 29ft 6in, and could accommodate ships of up to 300 tons. In the year 2000 the lock gates were replaced and the structure refurbished and stabilised at a cost of £500,000, funded in part by the EU, English Heritage and local councils. *Author's collection*

throughout. The lift up the inclines would be by continuous chains, mostly powered by water-wheels. The inclined planes would be at Marhamchurch, Venn, Merrifield, Tamerton, Werrington and Thurlibeer. The last-named was the largest, at 935 feet in length, raising the level of the canal by a full 225 feet. As built the canal was to be an impressive 35½ miles long, but at the huge cost of £120,000. An Act was passed in 1819 and a Bude Harbour & Canal Company was formed. The canal took six years to build, although part of it was opened after four years. The main canal ran from Bude to Blagdon Moor Wharf, near Holsworthy, and from a point called Red Post to Druxton Wharf, near Launceston, with a water feeder arm that ran from Tamar Lake. The Calstock objective was never achieved.

For more than 50 years the canal served its primary purpose but, with road improvements, the arrival of the railway at Holsworthy in 1879 (Bude 1898) and the production of chemical fertilisers, traffic declined rapidly. The canal effectively closed in 1884, but was not officially abandoned until 1891. It finally succumbed in 1902 when the undertaking was sold to the District Council. There were no mines, pits or quarries in the area and commercial vessels ceased using the canal basin in Edwardian times. Sand was carried from the beach to the canal basin by tramway between 1823 and 1942, with a change from 4-foot to 2-foot gauge in 1923. The old rails can still be seen, as illustrated. The basin survives and in 2000 the lock gates were replaced at a cost of £500,000.

The Bude Canal was the longest tub-boat canal in England, and was designed to carry lime-rich sea sand inland for agricultural purposes. Great use was made of inclined planes where the tub boats were chain-hauled up long slopes to gain altitude. The most significant of the inclines was 935 feet long and boats were raised 225 feet. The power was mainly provided by water-wheels. The sand tramway, seen here in 2001 at SS 204064, dates back to 1823; however, there was a change of gauge from 4 to 2 feet in 1923. In later years it was railway wagons rather than canal boats that were loaded with sand from the horse-drawn wagons. Operations ceased about 1942. *Author*

Shipping

Being surrounded by the sea it is hardly surprising that the Cornish have been involved with all things maritime since ancient times. Wooden sailing ships have been part of everyday Cornish life for centuries and it now seems amazing that at least since the 11th century ships from Cornwall were trading with Ireland, the rest of the UK and with ports from the Baltic to the Mediterranean. Prior to the advent of turnpike roads, tramways and railways in Cornwall every commodity being imported or exported in any volume was conveyed by ship. By 1833 there were 24,385 British-registered ships and this figure increased by more than 17% in the next seven years, rising to 28,692 by 1840 as the Industrial Revolution got under way, and Cornwall had more than its fair share of shipping registrations.

There were many different types of sailing ship, varying enormously in size and shape with a variety of rigging. In no particular order these ships fell into the categories of barge, cutter, ketch, lugger, gaffer, sloop, schooner, barque, brig, brigantine and barquentine, with fishing vessels carrying names that generally related to the type of fishing they indulged in, such as trawler, netter, crabber, seiner, scalloper, driver, ferry, etc. These names were further qualified to reflect their above-deck features, such as top-sail schooner, three-masted schooner, smack-rigged gaffer or sloop-rigged smack. Gradually iron-hulled ships appeared, especially of foreign manufacture. Later still steam-powered ships emerged and in the early days many steam ships had auxiliary sails. The word 'coaster' became part of the vocabulary, indicating a ship engaged on short

Prior to the arrival of the railways, and long before the roads of Cornwall were even approaching acceptable standards, the only way of transporting large volumes of minerals and merchandise was by ship. Invariably the ships were of wooden construction, powered by sail and ranging from 50-ton sloops and 175-ton three-masted schooners to 300-ton brigantines. Here some square-riggers are at anchor at Fowey waiting for loads. *Author's collection*

The larger the ship the greater its draught and consequently the deeper the water needed to be. In many small ports and those located in river estuaries or where tidal influences were extreme, only small vessels could be accommodated. Wadebridge, seen here, no longer handles cargo, but after the railway arrived from Wenford and Bodmin in 1833/4 until the line was extended to Padstow in 1899 it was a busy port, at least when the tide was high. Leaving the quayside in 1902 is the SS *Dunraven*, while in the background sailing ships can be seen on both sides of the River Camel. *Author's collection*

coastal runs around the UK or to the nearer European ports. Finally internal-combustion-engined motor vessels also began to appear, and some fully rigged sailing ships were fitted with oil engines, especially after the First World War.

Ignoring really small boats and fishing vessels, the Victorian version of the wooden sailing coaster could range from 30 to 250 tons, whereas the ocean-going vessels that often worked to the further Mediterranean ports and even across the Atlantic, to Newfoundland or South America, could be twice that size. Once the iron steam ships arrived in the late 19th century tonnage hugely increased and such ships could no longer enter ports such as Portreath or Newquay. Par could accept coasters of about 2,000 tons while the deep-water port of Fowey had no difficulty handling ships with a 12,000-ton displacement. At Falmouth enormous ships entered the port to shelter in Carrick Roads or to visit the dry docks.

In the perilous days of sail the number of casualties was unbelievable. In 1833 a total of 600 sailing ships were lost around the shores of the UK, and by 1866 a truly staggering 1,860 ships were lost, being either sunk, irreparably damaged or having simply disappeared. Some of these losses were dramatic, with ships being driven onto jagged rocks and smashed by heavy seas. These sensational events resulted in the loss of 1,500 lives every year, with all of the distress to families and communities that this caused. As we

In addition to freight there were also passengers to transport. In the early days passengers were sometimes carried on small commercial vessels with the absolute minimum in terms of facilities. However, on regular runs such as the link between the Cornish mainland and the Scilly Isles more appropriate ships were provided. In 1926 the Isles of Scilly Steamship Co Ltd took delivery of this steamship, the first *Scillonian*. Built in Scotland, she could carry 400 passengers as well as cargo. She is seen leaving the Scillies shortly after delivery. She was scrapped in about 1956. *Author's collection*

One of the most famous but now abandoned and silted-up ports was Devoran on Restronguet Creek (SX 796391). One of the great problems at Devoran was the regular silting up of the area by mining spoil travelling down the River Carnon and sea sand being deposited in the creek. The port developed as a result of the opening of the Redruth & Chasewater Railway in 1824/5, but once the Cornish mining era declined around 1908 the port handled only incoming coal and stone chippings for road building before falling into disuse. The railway closed in 1915 and the port died with it, the last load of coal arriving in 1916. The coaster *Erimus* of Falmouth leaves Devoran shortly before closure. *Author's collection*

In a typical modern scene at Newquay harbour, the small fishing vessel *Trevose* returns from a fishing trip, with shellfish being the primary catch. Although eking out a living from the sea is becoming more difficult, for generations Cornish culture has included all matters maritime.

Increasingly the sea is being used for recreational activities and at Newquay boat-owners and social sailors must take care to avoid jet skiers and surfers. Whatever the future holds, the days of commercial wooden sailing ships have gone forever. *Author*

will see in other chapters, lighthouses, coastguards and lifeboat services, combined with technological change in communications and equipment, would reduce but never eliminate loss of life in the shipping industry.

Most of the types of ship mentioned were designed and built with specific applications in mind. In tidal creeks, and where ships were beached to load and unload, there was a requirement for broad flat-bottomed hulls with a shallow draft. With some mid-size schooners the requirement was a combination of speed and manoeuvrability, while many of the largest ships sacrificed manoeuvrability and draft for sheer payload capacity. On the long-haul runs it was useful to have as much sail area as possible, but trying to negotiate a narrow harbour entrance with a 300-ton fully rigged sailing ship was cumbersome compared with a nimble 100-ton schooner. Also, in some areas it was easier to run aground with a large ship, especially in treacherous areas such as around Land's End, the Isles of Scilly, the Manacles Rocks or the infamous Doom Bar in the Camel estuary.

In the 20th century the construction of commercial vessels involved mainly metal ships, which required large shipbuilding dry docks, a fabrication capability, large cranes and a substantial specialised workforce. Shipbuilding in this era was confined mainly to large cities on major rivers where there was sufficient depth to launch ships weighing several thousand tons. However, the shipbuilding situation in Cornwall in the 19th century was very different. Nearly every Cornish port and estuary had a shipbuilding industry, where tiny

There are dozens of small and largely picturesque harbours dotted around the Cornish coast. Some, like Mevagissey and Padstow still retain a modicum of local fishing activity, although far from the scale of operations at Newlyn. However, for scores of small harbours 'messing about in boats' is as serious as it gets and the word 'shipping' is today a misnomer. One of these attractive ports is the delightfully named Mousehole, near Penzance, seen here in 1998. *Author*

shipyards would build small good-quality wooden ships. There were scores of shipyards all the way around the Cornish coast, and Newquay, for example, had more than its fair share.

There were four shipyards of note. The earliest, known as Clemen's Yard, was at Quay, within the inner harbour. It was run by the Clemen family from 1849 to 1869 and the first ship built was a schooner named *Treffry*, after the squire who owned the harbour. The sons of the family moved to nearby Island Cove Yard, below the cliffs just off Killacourt, and operated from there until 1871/2. The largest of the Clemen's yards was south of Newquay, the other side of the headland, at Tregunnel on the River Gannel. Another shipyard, owned by John Stephens and later Joseph Osborne, operated out of Porth, about a mile north of Newquay, until 1880. The last ship built in the area was in 1907.

The building of ships in Cornwall during the 19th century was promoted by the potential trade arising from the mining and china clay industries, which required a regular supply of shallow-draft vessels that could negotiate tidal creeks, coves and harbours. At the same time as these shipbuilding enterprises grew, organisations for the financing and managing of sailing fleets became established, forming shipping companies, with many local inhabitants getting a 'piece of the action' by investing therein. There was even a Newquay Maritime Association, effectively a marine insurance society. Many of the ships in the Newquay fleet were family owned and family manned, but this could have tragic results. For example, on 28 August 1874 the good ship *Josephine* was making its way from Cardiff to Newquay with a load of coal when it foundered in bad weather 1½ miles north-east of Trevose Head and the entire crew of four, who were all members of the Hockin family, were lost.

Mention must be made of the thousands of Cornish seafarers who manned the many hundreds of small wooden commercial ships and fishing boats plying for trade around the Cornish coastline up to and including the 19th century. Depending on their size, most of these small ships had a crew of between two and 12. Every ship had its 'Master', or Captain, and he was responsible for all aspects of running the ship, including scheduling based on tides, routing, navigating through difficult channels, avoiding severe weather, ensuring that provisions were adequate, ensuring his ship was not overloaded, and communicating with the ship-owners, customers, harbour masters, quayside employees and, of course, his crew. Sometimes his decisions were truly 'life or death'; the Master was responsible for all aspects of the safety of both his ship and its crew while operating in an often dangerous environment. Life as a seaman was tough. The work was heavy, the hours were long, and the conditions uncomfortable and above all dangerous. There was often no shelter on the open decks of the early vessels, leaving mariners to the ravages of the weather. The expression 'man overboard' was not invented in Hollywood! In fog the crew had to act as lookouts, not only for rocks but for larger passing ships, especially steamers in the later years. Often they would have to go aloft to attend to the sails and rigging, a very difficult job in cold and icy weather. In gales and storms it was often 'all hands on deck' to cope with the many essential tasks, which had to be accomplished in boots and oilskins. At other times ships could become becalmed, which required much patience. All of this had to be endured with sometimes poor rations and little sleep. Only the romantics will miss this now long-past era.

Shipwrecks

As just mentioned, being a mariner on a small wooden ship working around the Cornish coastline was a precarious business. On a fine summer's day with a gentle breeze, a calm sea, good visibility, a correctly loaded ship and a good skipper, there was little danger. However, as soon as any one of these factors changed, the greater the odds of a problem occurring. Statistically 30% of Cornish ships were lost between April and September and 70% between October and March, so nobody could argue that the weather was not the most significant factor in contributing to shipwrecks and therefore casualties.

The casualty statistics are simply mind-boggling. In Padstow alone, one medium-sized Cornish port out of dozens, more than 500 19th-century ships were lost. If those figures are extrapolated to include the whole of the county, then the figure would be in the thousands. Nationally, one in every 40 ships was lost every year. In 1866, for example, 1,842 ships and some 900 lives were lost, despite the lifeboat service allegedly saving 1,600 lives. Gradually, as rescue services, equipment and technology improved, the number of losses decreased, but on the rugged coasts of Cornwall even steam ships with metal hulls and giant contemporary supertankers are still vulnerable. For example, the famous *Torrey Canyon* disaster occurred on 18 March 1967 when, due to navigational confusion on board, a supertanker carrying 120,000 tons of crude oil from Kuwait to Milford Haven struck Pollard's Rock on the infamous Seven Stones Reef between the Scilly Isles and the Cornish mainland. The ship was nearly 1,000 feet long and some 125 feet wide. It could not be re-floated and it broke

4 ROUGH SEA. ST. MAWES

Unless one has experienced a full Atlantic gale during winter it is hard to imagine the hardship, rigours, perils and the power of the sea. Such conditions would be uncomfortable in a cruise ship, but experiencing them in a sail-powered 150-ton wooden schooner, with limited navigational aids and no satellite-generated weather warnings, would be a very different matter. This locally produced postcard shows mountainous seas smashing over the seafront at St Mawes. *Author's collection*

up on the rocks, with massive oil spillage. The entire operation was a disaster, with toxic detergents being used to disperse the oil, a salvage worker being killed and an estimated 15,000 seabirds perishing along 120 miles of heavily polluted Cornish coastline.

It is now hard to imagine being a crew member on a 100-ton wooden schooner, in the darkness of a cold January night, with gale-force winds battering the creaking and rolling vessel, the minimum of shelter, no radio communication, no engine to power into or out of the storm and only monstrous waves and high jagged rocks to feed the imagination. Flares or sightings by the coastguard were the only salvation, other than rapidly making for a harbour of refuge where the ship could ride out the storm. As already mentioned, in later years lighthouses appeared and the coastguard and lifeboat services were established, but even those brave souls could not always save life. Indeed, in researching this subject the most harrowing stories were instances where a ship left a harbour and was never seen or heard from again.

There have been more than a thousand shipwrecks off the Cornish coast, and some will live forever in folklore, either because of the fame of the ship or due to a particularly large loss of life. For example, on 7 May 1875 the German liner SS *Schiller* was wrecked on Retarrier Ledge on the Isles of Scilly and 335 passengers and crew perished. There follows a representative sample of lesser losses, in no particular order.

The ketch *Amelia* was built in Penzance in 1820, and in September 1850 she was wrecked off Ilfracombe while carrying coal and iron. The Master survived but was reprimanded for trying to enter the harbour at night and in fog. The ship was repaired but was 'presumed lost' in September 1858. The schooner *Ann Williams* was built in Padstow in 1864 and worked out of Port Isaac. She was wrecked in a great storm at the Black Dog, near Aberdeen, in March 1881, and only one of her crew of seven survived. The schooner *Annie*, built at Padstow in 1863, was wrecked at St Tudwal's Island 14 years later; the crew of five were all saved by the Abersoch lifeboat, but the ship was lost. The sloop-rigged smack *Bee* was built at Appledore in 1846. In March 1880 she was nearing Bude with a cargo of culm from Swansea when very strong winds drove her ashore. The ship broke up but the entire crew were able to walk ashore. The schooner *Bessie*, registered at Truro, worked out of Devoran for many years. She set sail from Glasgow on 23 October 1909 with a load of coal for Charlestown and was never heard from again; it is assumed that she and her crew of five were lost at sea.

The renamed sloop *Boscastle* was built in France and between 1810 and 1815 she worked out of the tiny harbour of the same name. She was lost with all hands off Aberthaw in February 1815 while sailing from Boscastle to Bristol. The schooner *Carrie* was a very unlucky ship; built at Truro in 1878, she encountered a storm off St Ann's Head in February 1899 on her way to Milford Haven. Two hands came on deck to find the Mate's body jammed in the port rail and the Master lying in the aft hold with a broken neck. The ship reached Milford with the two dead bodies on board. The deceased master, T. Solomon, lived at Newquay and left a wife and five children. Four years later in March 1903 a message

Sailing ships were particularly vulnerable to bad weather, but experienced skippers would aim for a harbour of refuge at the first sign of potentially damaging gales, especially if heavily laden with cargo. Even steam ships suffered, especially when there was any form of mechanical breakdown. The SS *Castleford* has come to grief on the Western Rocks on the Isles of Scilly in June 1887, but remains largely intact. *Cornish Studies Library*

The entire Cornish coastline is littered with shipwrecks. In days of old some wooden ships were literally shattered on the rocks and washed-up cargo would often be plundered by the local population. There was heavy loss of life on a regular basis. In this dramatic view, the SS *City of Cardiff* has been driven onto rocks at Nanjizal (Mill Bay), near Land's End, in heavy seas on 21 March 1912. A member of crew is being rescued by breeches buoy and can be seen above the treacherous surf. *Cornish Studies Library*

was received at Penzance coastguard station that the *Carrie* had struck the Runnelstone and the crew of four had taken to their small lifeboat, which drifted towards Porthwarra. In terrible seas the Captain was washed out of the boat, and as they approached the rugged coast the other three leapt out, to avoid being smashed on the rocks. Only Duncan Mackenzie climbed the cliff and the other two were never seen again.

The *Celerity* was built in 1839 and lengthened in 1848. She worked out of Penzance and often to Mediterranean ports and the Azores. Ironically she was lost off Holyhead in December 1852 with no survivors. In contrast, the schooner *Cornish Lass* had a long life. Built in Padstow in 1841, she worked out of St Ives between 1846 and 1896. However, at 55 years of age her luck ran out when she was trying to enter St Agnes with a load of coal from Lydney. She was driven onto Trevellas Rocks and became a total loss; the fate of her crew is not known. The suitably named smack *Delabole* was built at Padstow but changed

ports often, being owned successively by operators at Port Isaac, Falmouth and Fowey. On 16 September 1880 she was taking a load of Luxulyan granite from Par to Swansea when she was lost off Clovelly. Her crew of three were all saved by the Clovelly lifeboat.

Although there may well have been a handful of instances, it is largely a myth that local inhabitants waved lamps from

Heavy seas could produce waves of 40 to 50 feet or more and they would crash over the decks of small craft. Over the years lighthouses were positioned on the more important headlands and near dangerous reefs and rocks; in addition, the coastguard and later the lifeboat services were on hand at specific locations to help seafarers. In this view the *Eureka* has been driven onto Lauggan Rocks near Penzance Beach; St Michael's Mount can just be made out through the storm. *Cornish Studies Library*

the shore to lure ships onto the rocks. However, what is demonstrably true is the plundering of cargo from almost every shipwreck along the coast, and the removal of any valuable fixtures and fittings from the stricken vessel was widespread. The seabed around Cornwall is littered with the remains of ships and over the years wreck-diving has become a popular pastime. However, even without being superstitious or believing in the supernatural, one cannot help but think that the ghosts of all those poor drowned seafarers from past centuries are not far away!

Lighthouses

To provide some sort of navigational aid fishermen in the Middle Ages paid to have beacons lit at night at certain strategic points around the coast. However, this was piecemeal and completely ineffective, particularly in adverse climatic conditions. Although progress was slow, during the 17th century lighthouses started to be built on groups of rocks and on selected headlands in an attempt to reduce the appalling number of shipwrecks, and responsibility was vested in the Trinity House association.

The lighthouses that were located on rocks surrounded by sea were extremely difficult to construct. For example, when Wolf Rock lighthouse was being built only 83 hours of work were possible in an entire year! Foundation pits were dug in solid rock by using hand drills, picks and hammers. The large granite stones used in construction were cut and shaped on land and loaded into special barges. At the lighthouse a simple crane

This remarkable postcard, postally used in 1935, shows just how vulnerable shipping can be as vessels of every size round Land's End. In the distance, 1¼ miles offshore, is Longships lighthouse and between it and the rocks two steamships can be seen ploughing westward through the shipping channel. The famous lighthouse has a powerful light with a range of 19 miles but, like all Cornish lighthouses, is now unmanned. *Author's collection*

Pendeen lighthouse, between St Ives and Land's End, photographed in March 2007, is located on the top of cliffs on Cornwall's north coast. Established in the year 1900 its light has a range of 16 nautical miles and the tower is 17 metres high. The former lightkeeper's accommodation block is now used for holiday lets. On site are two enormous fog warning horns that are still operational. The earliest record of lights to help shipping was in 1396 when 'beaconage' was paid for by fisherman to keep a light burning at the chapel on the top of Carn Brea Hill. *Author*

would be used to unload the stone, which would then be winched into position. The slender structures could be 150 feet high with eight levels and 70 layers of stone. Over the years many Cornish lighthouses have had to be rebuilt and in some cases replaced. The lighthouses on cliff tops were generally shorter than the towers at sea.

In the early days the primary light source comprised a wood- or coal-burning brazier; the original lighthouse at the Lizard had two towers and therefore two fires. Another option was magnified candle power, used in Devon's Eddystone lighthouses. In 1782 an oil-fed wick was used for the first time. For more than a hundred years this early technology developed, resulting in multiple concentric wicks that produced a brighter light. The oil originally used was fish oil and later vegetable and mineral oil. In 1901 the adoption of a pressurised oil feed combined with an incandescent mantle tripled the previous light output. Lens technology also improved when a Fresnel lens was placed in front of the light source. Later, still lights were mounted on a revolving mechanism, enabling a lighthouse to transmit its own distinctive light pattern. Eventually electricity was used to the exclusion of all else, supplied either from generators or from the mains. The power rating of each lighthouse varies, but a range of about 24 nautical miles is not unusual.

The impact of poor weather on the manning of lighthouses cannot be understated. At rocky seabound locations keepers could spend a month on a lighthouse without a relief crew being able to land. Men and supplies were often winched off the rocks using a small crane and usually each crew comprised three men, one being on duty for 8 hours

St Anthony's lighthouse (SW 846311) has protected shipping from Manacle Rocks, near Falmouth, since 1835. It was converted to electric lighting as recently as 1954 and was automated in 1987. Its 1,500-watt lamp, suitably magnified, has a range of 22 nautical miles. There were normally three lighthouse keepers who worked shifts to man the lighthouse 24 hours a day, 365 days a year. This lighthouse was notable for its huge bell (visible in this old view) rather than a conventional foghorn. *Author's collection*

St. Anthony's Lighthouse, Falmouth

per day. Lighthouses normally comprised eight floors with a room of approximately 12 feet at each level. Three levels were used as living accommodation, usually comprising a kitchen, living room and bedroom. The toilet normally consisted of a bucket that was emptied into the sea! By the 1980s a programme to fully automate every lighthouse was instigated and none of Cornwall's lighthouses are now manned, although there are occasional maintenance visits.

Lighthouses in Cornwall and the Isles of Scilly, all west of Eddystone lighthouse (located on a rock at Rame Head, 8 miles from Plymouth) are:

St Anthony	(1835) on the shore by the entrance to Falmouth Harbour
Lizard	(rebuilt 1752) on Lizard Point
Tater Du	(1965) east of Land's End
Round Island	(1887) Isles of Scilly
Peninnis light	(1910) at St Mary's
Bishop Rock	(1858, strengthened in 1887) 45 metres high, on the westernmost tip of the Scillies
Wolf Rock	(1862) 8 miles from Land's End
Longships	(1795) on a rock 1¼ miles off Land's End
Pendeen	(1900) on the cliff tops between Land's End and St Ives
Godrevy	(1858) on an island in St Ives Bay
Trevose	(1847) on cliffs south of Padstow

There is also Sevenstones Lightship, anchored off Sevenstones Reef, 10 miles north-east of the Scillies.

The lighthouse at Trevose Head (SX 850766) stands on top of 150-foot-high cliffs and commands spectacular views. The building dates back to 1847 and it was manned until 1995. In 1514 King Henry VIII founded Trinity House, which was responsible for pilot boats around the UK's shores. Responsibilities were later extended to the building, operating and maintaining of lighthouses. Trevose is the most northerly of Cornwall's lighthouses, seen here in September 2003. *Author*

Lifeboats and coastguards

With the unacceptably high number of shipwrecks around the British coast and a commensurate loss of life, a 'National Institute for the Preservation of Life from Shipwrecks' was formed in 1824, its origins being on the Isle of Man. Thirty years later the name was changed to the 'Royal National Lifeboat Institution', or RNLI as it is popularly known today. Over the decades the institution expanded to 233 lifeboat stations, working 332 lifeboats and with 4,600 volunteer crew members on call. A number of the older stations have been closed over the years.

The work of the RNLI has substantially changed in recent decades. While there are still dozens of shipwrecks around our coasts every year the totals are but a fraction of the disasters that occurred during the days of sail. Iron steam ships were still vulnerable to the vagaries of the weather and mechanical failure, but on nothing like the same scale as their wooden predecessors. Even modern motor vessels, with all their safety features and sophisticated radar and communications equipment, are not immune from disaster, but with the immense growth in the leisure industry it is now more likely to be a weekend sailor in his small yacht who is in need of rescue or assistance. Also, those indulging in a wide range of water sports are regularly the subject of rescues, and for these the RNLI has five classes of inshore

Above: Although the statistic is hard to believe, in 1842 no fewer than 600 ships were lost around the shores of the British Isles, and a staggering 1,500 seamen lost their lives each year while performing their normal duties. Eventually the Royal National Lifeboat Institution was formed to save lives, but even the RNLI has had its share of disasters. During 1981 the entire eight-man crew of the Penlee lifeboat, the *Solomon Browne*, was tragically drowned when attempting the rescue of the coaster *Union Star*, which was also lost with eight hands on board. The new 40-tonne 2,500bhp 'Severn' class Penlee lifeboat is seen at Newlyn in 2007. *Author*

Left: Not all lifeboat stations are easily accessed by land, and the new RNLI installation at the Lizard has gone to elaborate lengths to ensure that supplies reach the station by providing a fairly sophisticated funicular railway, seen here on 12 July 2007. There are now eight main lifeboat stations in Cornwall and a further four so-called 'inshore' lifeboats at other sites. Falmouth and St Ives have both types of craft. *M. Dart*

Many old lifeboat stations that used the 'slip' principle to launch their craft have been abandoned. The steepest slip was located at Newquay, but it closed as long ago as 1934. More recent victims (by way of example) that have fallen into disuse are located at Penlee, Hawker's Cove near Padstow and the Lizard, seen here in derelict condition in March 1997. The slip superstructure has fallen into the sea and the roof is starting to disintegrate. *Author*

lifeboat, including inflatables, and six classes of all-weather high-speed lifeboats for deeper waters.

The RNLI continues to perform a vital function and on average 22 people a day are rescued from precarious situations. These occurrences vary from major incidents in heavy seas to towing small vessels with mechanical or equipment problems into harbour and rescuing those who have floated out to sea on inflatables or on surfboards and are at risk of drowning. Some rescues have been on a colossal scale. In 1907 the 12,000-ton liner SS *Suevic* hit Maenheere Reef off Lizard Point and over a period of 16 hours 456 passengers and crew were rescued by four lifeboats from Cadgwith, Coverack, the Lizard and Porthleven. Throughout history the lifeboats themselves have been vulnerable and

On Lifeboat Days and certain Bank Holidays the local lifeboat was always a part of the proceedings and various demonstrations drew in the crowds, albeit from a public that was perhaps more easily entertained in those far-off days. In this touched-up Edwardian picture the Newquay lifeboat *James Stevens No 5* hits the water with some force as the crowds look on in awe. In 1908 the lifeboat capsized on exercise resulting in the loss of one Harry Storey. *Author's collection*

Above: This most wonderful relic can easily be found on Towan Head at Newquay; the remains of the 1895 lifeboat slipway, which, at a gradient of 1 in 2¼ was the steepest ever built in the UK. The boat was wheeled across an access road from the boathouse and tipped onto the slipway. This shallow trough guided the ridge on the bottom of the boat's hull down to the water. The station was closed in 1934 and the slip was never used again. This view was recorded in April 2007, at SX 801628. *Author*

there have been disasters on a significant scale.

Such tragedies are not confined to the Victorian era. As recently as 19 December 1981 the Penlee lifeboat was lost with all hands while trying to rescue the Dublin-registered *Union Star*. The latter ship was on its maiden voyage from the Netherlands to Ireland with a cargo of fertiliser; it had five crew members on board together with the Captain's wife and their two daughters. The *Union Star* developed an engine fault 8 miles east of Wolf Rock, but the Captain, Henry Morton, was not prepared to accept a tow because under the Lloyds Open Form salvage contract he might have to pay an undetermined amount for salvage. The weather worsened and the winds increased to 80mph, gusting to a hurricane-force 95mph. The ship's fuel supply became contaminated by seawater and any chance of restarting the engine disappeared as the ship was driven towards rocks at Boscawen Cove, near Lamora. The stricken ship gave out a distress signal to the Coastguard at Falmouth but conditions were so bad that RNAS Culdrose could not fly its Sea King helicopter. The Penlee lifeboat was launched with a crew of 12, all from

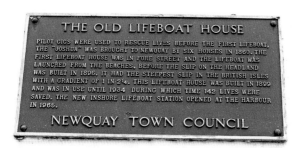

THE OLD LIFEBOAT HOUSE

PILOT GIGS WERE USED TO RESCUE LIVES BEFORE THE FIRST LIFEBOAT.
THE "JOSHUA" WAS BROUGHT TO NEWQUAY BY SIX HORSES IN 1860. THE
FIRST LIFEBOAT HOUSE WAS IN FORE STREET AND THE LIFEBOAT WAS
LAUNCHED FROM THE BEACHES. BEFORE THE SLIP ON THE HEADLAND
WAS BUILT IN 1895. IT. HAD THE STEEPEST SLIP IN THE BRITISH ISLES
WITH A GRADIENT OF 1 IN 2¼. THIS LIFEBOAT HOUSE WAS BUILT IN 1899
AND WAS IN USE UNTIL 1934. DURING WHICH TIME 142 LIVES WERE
SAVED. THE NEW INSHORE LIFEBOAT STATION OPENED AT THE HARBOUR
IN 1965.

NEWQUAY TOWN COUNCIL

This self-explanatory sign is affixed to the surviving 1899-built RNLI boathouse on the Headland at Newquay. What the sign does not say is that the Newquay station was reopened as a wartime measure from 1940 to 1945, with the lifeboat located in the harbour, where the new inshore station has been located since 1965. A brand-new boathouse was completed at the harbour in 1994. *Author*

This colourful pair of RNLI lifeboats were photographed in the Camel estuary in September 2006. No 14-29 is a 27.5-tonne 'Trent' class lifeboat and No 16-01 is a 31.5-tonne 'Tamar' class. The first true lifeboat at Padstow was the *Mariner's Friend*, built by one John Tredwen in 1827; the first RNLI vessel arrived in 1856, a six-oared boat named *Albert Edward*, after the Duke of Cornwall, who contributed £25 towards the cost. *Author*

the village of Mousehole. The conditions were atrocious with huge seas, yet the lifeboat managed to get alongside and rescue four people; it then returned for the others, but this proved fatal. A huge 60-foot wave threw the lifeboat *Solomon Browne* up and over the *Union Star* and it is thought that the lifeboat was smashed onto the rocks in the cove. Other lifeboats tried to reach the spot but both vessels were lost. Only eight of the 16 bodies were ever found, and the wreckage of the lifeboat was eventually found strewn along the shore. The present Penlee lifeboat works out of Newlyn rather than the old slip at Penlee Point.

Main lifeboat stations are at Fowey, Falmouth, Lizard, Penlee (Newlyn), Sennen Cove, St Ives and Padstow, with additional inshore stations at St Agnes, Newquay, Port Isaac and Bude. Closed stations were at Looe, Polkerris, Mevagissey, Portloe, Porthoustock, Coverack, Cadgwith, Church Cove, Mullion, Porthleven, Penzance and Hayle.

The coastguard service now co-ordinates all rescues and decides which of the rescue services to call. The service goes back more than 200 years when it was mainly concerned with looking out for smugglers and keeping an eye open from the cliff tops for Napoleonic invasion forces. In many parts of Cornwall there are small rows of terraced houses, normally on the coastline, which are often called 'Coastguard Cottages', where the coastguards once lived. In 1831 the Admiralty had fostered the coastguard service as a naval reserve, but the main activities were life-saving, overseeing and securing the salvage from wrecks and administering the foreshore. The service made a significant contribution in both World Wars. By 1923 it was part of the Board of Trade, and in 1990 it became a Government Executive Agency. After various amalgamations in 1998 the Maritime and Coastguard Agency was formed.

All maritime matters and rescue activities in Cornwall are controlled from a communications station at Falmouth, one of 19 dotted around the UK coast. The coastguard remains an on-call 24-hours-a-day emergency organisation responsible for the initiation of Search and Rescue (SAR) activities within the UK. It has its own SAR capability and works in co-operation with the Air Sea Rescue services provided by the Royal Navy and the Royal Air Force. It is also alert to missing persons, potential threats to maritime pollution and accident prevention. Its spectrum of activity includes everything from serious illness at sea to exhausted sailboarders and even walkers who have fallen from cliffs. Gone are the days of feeble flares and cries from the sea – nowadays a satellite in space is more likely to identify a problem.

In a county such as Cornwall, with its many rivers, estuaries, peninsulas and inlets, especially on the south coast, it was inevitable that crossing from one side to the other would involve travelling by boat. Where there was a demand for regular travel, boat-owners started to provide a service for a fee. Some ferry crossings are truly ancient but even 'modern' innovations such as the Saltash and Torpoint chain ferries date back to 1833 and 1834 respectively! One of the ancient crossings is from Bodinnick to Fowey, and in March 2007 the current ferry, with vehicle ramps at each end, is seen crossing the River Fowey. *Author*

The crossing of the River Fal at Carrick Roads, south of Truro, has been established since the Middle Ages, with evidence showing such an operation in the 15th century. In 1888 services were taken over by the King Harry Steam Ferry Company and the company is now owned by five local families. Since 1888 there have been just seven ferries in service. Steam power was ousted by diesel in 1956. This scene from the 1950s shows cars of the period on board; one of the guiding chains can be seen on the right of the vessel as she runs from Philleigh to Feock. *Author's collection*

Ferries

A journey by road along the southern coast of Cornwall centuries ago, before turnpike roads were established, was interrupted by the many inlets and estuaries along the way and a part-journey by ferry was commonplace. The most important ferry crossing, certainly in terms of usage, was across the River Tamar, because other than a few ancient bridges above Gunnislake there were no road crossings across the mighty river. These ferries provided the only transport link between Devon (and the rest of England) and Cornwall, except in the north of the county. From the 15th century ferry rights at Cremyll were owned by the Earl of Mount Edgecumbe and the ferry service substantially pre-dates that era!

The two major ferry crossings across the Tamar were at Saltash and at Torpoint, opened as chain ferries in 1833 and 1834 respectively. The ferries were called 'floating bridges' and they were driven by steam and later diesel engines linked to the chains, a method of propulsion that still survives. Both were designed by the engineer James Rendel, who had designed similar operations at other south-coast locations. After operating for 128 years the Saltash Ferry ceased operation in 1961, when the new road suspension bridge was opened beside Brunel's famous 1859 Royal Albert Bridge.

The Torpoint Ferry can be traced back to 1791, and almost 220 years later this major crossing now has a busy three-ferry operation. Back in 1922 the owners were struggling financially and the business was acquired by Cornwall County Council, which then ran the ferries, later in conjunction with Plymouth City Council, under joint committee control. The old and basic steam-powered floating bridges were finally replaced by diesel power in the 1960s and at the same time a third arrived. The new ferries, the *Lynher*, *Tamar* and *Plym*, operated for about 40 years until replaced in 2004-6 by three new floating bridges. At this time a new road configuration and control tower were built to help eliminate the fearful peak-period traffic queues with which the operation had become associated. The new vessels were faster, quieter and 50% bigger than their predecessors. The current ferries have a 73-car capacity, are about 240 feet long and 67 feet wide, are powered by 12-litre Volvo Penta engines, and each cost £4.9 million to build. The new operation was inaugurated by HRH The Princess Royal on 28 April 2007. The Torpoint Ferry is open 24 hours a day, 365 days a year, with a 10-minute-interval service at peak periods, and carries 2 million vehicles per annum, the busiest estuarial vehicular crossing in the UK.

Many small ferries operate throughout Cornwall, for example across the East Looe River, from Fowey to Polruan, at Malpas, south of Truro, and from Percuil and St Mawes to St Anthony, Flushing and Falmouth, across Helford Passage and from Rock

A brand-new chain ferry was acquired in 2006, which is seen here working towards King Harry's cottages on the Feock side of the River Fal. Called simply No 7, the ferry can carry 34 cars and during the course of a year it is estimated that it saves motorists some 5 million road miles. Both chains can be seen beyond the gorse bushes. During winter weekdays the last ferry presently runs at 19.30 from the Roseland side of the river. *Author*

The history of the Saltash Ferry dates back to 1066 when, until the year 1270, it was operated by the Vellefort family. Inflation followed, with the Burgesses of Saltash paying an annual rent to the Duchy of Cornwall of £10 in 1337 and £20 in 1618! In 1929 32,400 passengers were carried per annum. With the Royal Albert Bridge as a backdrop, the chain ferry is seen here in 1924 with both horse and motor vehicle traffic visible. The last ferry ran in October 1961 when the new Tamar road bridge was opened. *Author's collection*

to Padstow. There are many ferry services in and around the Isles of Scilly, which although not part of Cornwall are worth mentioning. Then there are many other summer and tidal services, such as summer trips from Plymouth to Calstock on the Tamar, from Mevagissey to Fowey and, on high tides, from Fowey to Lerryn.

Two other ferries with an ancient tradition are the Bodinnick Ferry to Fowey and the King Harry Ferry from Feock to Philleigh on the Roseland peninsula. The Bodinnick Ferry was once on the important Torpoint to Falmouth route and has been in operation for centuries. In days of old the shallow barge-like ferry was rowed across the River Fowey by two men using large sweeps, or long paddles. The route was slightly changed

The Torpoint Ferry, seen here in 2007, remains a vital link between Devon and Cornwall, and recently £3 million has been invested in three new vessels. Each of these impressive vessels can carry 73 cars. Lorries and buses also use the ferry services; indeed, the ferry was claimed to be the only floating bus fare stage in the UK! The peak service provides for a ferry departure every 10 minutes and the business is run in conjunction with the Tamar road bridge. *Author*

in 1977 when, on the Fowey side of the river, the ferry was moved from the awkward Passage Slip to Caffa Mill Pill, where there was more room for cars. In 2001 the old vehicle floats were replaced by a self-propelled double-ended vehicle ferry.

The King Harry Ferry across the River Fal has a history that goes back more than 500 years. An old barge-style man-powered ferry was replaced in 1888 when the King Harry Steam Ferry Co Ltd was formed. In the intervening 120 years only seven ferries have been used: 1889-1913, 1913-50, 1950 only, 1950-62, 1962-74, 1974-2006, and 2006-date. Steam propulsion ended in 1956. The ferry runs on 364 days of the year, makes about 80 crossings per day and transports in total 280,000 cars per annum. A car journey by ferry, for anybody who would otherwise travel by road via Truro, saves 27 miles. The new 2006 ferry is chain-driven, weighs 350 tonnes, carries 34 cars and cost £2.8 million.

Finally, one of the significant ferry journeys operated by larger conventional vessels is from Penzance to St Mary's on the Isles of Scilly. With the coming of the railway to Penzance in the mid-19th century, demand for a reliable steamer service to the Scilly Isles increased. The West Cornwall Steamship Co Ltd was formed by two Directors of the West Cornwall Railway in 1871 to improve the reliability of steamship services, which had been in operation for some years. In 1875 one of the Scilly steamers, *Lady of the Isles*, was built in Cornwall by Harveys of Hayle. Ships came and went but in 1926

One of the major problems facing the mine-owners in the late 18th and early 19th centuries was the transportation of the output from the mines to ports for shipment, mainly to South Wales where the ore would be smelted. There was an inlet at Portreath, a mile or two north of Basset's Cove, named after the influential Basset family who owned it. They created an artificial harbour at this north-coast location and in 1809 the first lengthy horse-powered tramway in Cornwall was constructed, linking the port with the mining districts at Poldice and later St Day. A remarkable survivor is the 'Directors coach' from that era, now housed in the Royal Cornwall Museum in Truro. *M. Dart*

the first of a series of ships to carry the name *Scillonian* was delivered. Built in Glasgow, the ship could carry 400 passengers. The second *Scillonian* arrived from its Southampton builders in 1956, powered by two Ruston & Hornsby diesel engines. A *Scillonian III* arrived from its Appledore builders in 1977; weighing 1,255 tons, she could carry 600 passengers and is still a regular sight docking at Penzance.

Portreath

The man-made harbour at Portreath was historically significant in that it was the first harbour in Cornwall to be rail-connected to its primary customers for the transportation of goods and minerals. The ancient harbour area was the fishing port of the Manor of Trehidy, the home of the influential Basset family. However, in the late 18th and early 19th centuries copper mining in the St Day and Gwennap areas was expanding so rapidly that something had to be done about the mineral transportation problem. It was becoming increasingly difficult to transport large volumes of heavy ore to the ports by mule, horse or early primitive wagons and to convey backloads of coal.

Accordingly the Bassets embarked upon the construction of a permanent harbour where ships could berth, and £12,000 was spent on a pier, jetty and warehouses before the entire harbour was leased to an operating company owned in part by the Fox family of Falmouth and the Williams family of Scorrier House. This company made further improvements, spending a further £6,000 on an inner basin, making Portreath the most important north coast harbour between Newquay and Hayle. With a dredged channel, proper granite quays and a protective harbour wall, medium-sized ships began to call. In addition, it was proposed to build a five and a half mile tramway of approximately 3ft 6in gauge, whereby horse-drawn wagons would travel on long L-shaped cast-iron plates tied to granite setts or sleepers. The cost would be £20,000, a significant sum in 1808.

Lord de Dunstanville laid the first rail in October 1809 and, when complete, the tramway would be the first of its kind in Cornwall. By 1812 the single-track line was opened as far as North Downs and Scorrier House to serve the St Day and Treskerby mining area, and in 1816 it was extended to Crofthandy, to serve the vast Poldice mining complex. The line was an immediate commercial success and business was

The old Poldice Tramway (also known as the Portreath Tramway) was the forerunner of many mineral lines. The first rail was laid by Lord de Dunstanville in October 1809. The approximately 3ft 6in gauge line comprised L-shaped rails attached to square-shaped granite blocks or setts. It survived until the great mining crash of 1865 when there was a severe slump in worldwide commodity prices. This surviving tunnel is where the tramway ran under the West Cornwall Railway's main line at Scorrier (SW 722442). *Author*

By 1837 the Hayle Railway wanted a piece of the Portreath action and opened a standard-gauge branch line extending 3 miles 4 chains from its Hayle to Redruth main line. The line was straightforward in construction except the final approach to the harbour, which required a half-mile 1 in 7 incline. From 1865 the branch provided the only rail connection to Portreath, and although it survived several depressions in the mining industry it finally closed from 1 January 1936. This photograph shows the line at the end of its days at Illogan. *Brunel University, Clinker Collection*

booming. By 1840 the small harbour was shipping 100,000 tons of copper ore representing more than 700 shiploads per annum and importing vast quantities of coal. There was even a 'domestic' shipping company, D. W. Bain & Co, operating 18 schooners out of Portreath.

In the early 1830s the Hayle Railway was planning its line from Hayle to Tresavean Mine with branches to Redruth and Portreath. Acts passed in 1834 and 1836 gave the Hayle Railway Company necessary approvals, with a capital of £64,000 and powers to borrow a

small ports on the north coast were notoriously difficult to enter during periods of inclement weather, especially in the days of sail. However, they were much nearer to South Wales, to where the ore was shipped and from where coal was brought. Once the Cornish main line opened throughout from Saltash to Penzance less use was made of Portreath. The port once had a

thriving fishing industry and in 1880 one Portreath-based company owned no fewer than 16 registered fishing vessels. However, as ships became larger they could not enter the port, resulting in terminal decline. By 1900 there were only about 200 shipping movements per year. In this circa 1913 view three steam ships are in the port. *P. Q. Treloar collection*

further £16,000 if necessary. The line to Portreath, 3 miles 4 chains long, was straightforward to construct, except for the final descent to Portreath Harbour by means of a 1 in 7 inclined plane. Good progress was made and the Portreath branch was opened throughout on 23 December 1837, giving the port the benefit of two rail routes. This standard-gauge branch was later worked by the West Cornwall Railway and the Great Western Railway.

There was a major recession in the mining industry during the mid-1860s and by this time the main line from Plymouth to Penzance was open. The Poldice Mine had become exhausted in the late 1850s and this fatal combination of events spelled the end for the old Poldice Tramway (sometimes called the Portreath tramway). By 1866 copper ore production had halved, and in the following year 7,000 unemployed miners and their families emigrated all over the world. There was a mild recovery in the following years and it is said that on one day in May 1873 there were 20 vessels, including three steamers, in the harbour. On the quayside was a lime kiln and coal dumps, as well as mobile cranes. For several decades wagons were raised and lowered on the cable-worked incline, accessing the harbour via small single-wagon-length turntables. Rail traffic gradually petered out and coastal ships became too large to use the harbour. Eventually even the domestic coal business failed and the line at Portreath closed on 1 January 1936.

The remains of the old incline can still be seen at SW 657452, but otherwise the harbour area has been completely redeveloped with housing all around the old inner basin. The harbour wall is, of course, still in situ, but Portreath is now a 'lost port'.

Calstock

It was natural for settlements to be established along a river, especially one as important as the part-navigable River Tamar, which provides a natural boundary between Devon and Cornwall. There was certainly a quay at Calstock in Saxon times, but archaeologists have dated mining in the area back to Roman times. Once large-scale mineral deposits were discovered in the late 18th century there was the usual need for good transportation and access to ships and the sea. The village of Calstock was perfectly situated to capture the output from the many local mines. However, there was one significant problem: Calstock was at river level and most of the mines were on high ground. It was expensive and hazardous to transport materials by packhorse and later horse and cart on steeply graded unmetalled roads, especially in poor weather during the winter months.

Mining in the area was at its zenith in the early 1860s and in 1862 the Tamar, Kit Hill & Callington Railway was formed to build a 7-mile railway from Callington to Calstock Quay, featuring an inclined plane up from Kelly Quay, Calstock, to higher ground. Work started on the line in 1863/4 but the 1866 slump in the international mining industry resulted in insufficient finance being made available to complete the line. A further attempt was made in 1869, but this time a 3ft 6in gauge was chosen. Progress was rapid and the freight-only narrow-gauge line opened from Calstock to Callington on 8 May 1872. An 1871 Act saw the name changed to the East Cornwall Minerals Railway. Two narrow-gauge locomotives were employed and a stationary steam engine worked the incline, with horses being used for shunting on the quay. The inclined plane was single track, just under half a mile long with a passing loop halfway up the 1 in 6 gradient;

This early Edwardian scene, recorded before the railway viaduct was built across the river in 1907, shows a very commercial River Tamar at Calstock. Five sailing ships, the SS *Albion* and a small paddle-steamer are visible in this busy scene. There are railway wagons on the quay that have descended to the quayside via the East Cornwall Minerals Railway incline, seen in the left middle distance. The output was from a large number of mines and quarries in the Hingston Downs area, including Kit Hill, was shipped from Kelly Quay, Calstock. *M. Dart collection*

it raised the level of the railway by 350 feet. The ECMR was an immediate success, the only limitation being the size of ship that could reach Calstock, where the quays had 450 yards of rail-served moorings. At the turn of the 20th century paddle-steamers were a common sight and steamship coasters would navigate their way up the River Tamar to collect granite and bricks, while the famous Tamar sailing barges were part of the local maritime scene (the 1899-built barge *Shamrock* is preserved at the nearby Cotehele Quay).

The ECMR continued to be successful, and in 1894 the Plymouth, Devonport & South Western Junction Railway took it over. In collaboration with the London & South Western Railway, authority was sought to build a standard-gauge branch line from Bere Alston to Callington, approval being given in 1905. The famous Colonel Stephens was appointed engineer of the line. The River Tamar would have to be crossed on a 12-arch, 120-foot-high, 870-foot-long viaduct, and in total four 'new' miles of track would be required before the new line joined the old ECMR alignment. Calstock Viaduct was an impressive structure and dominated the village below it, while the village's station was located just on the Cornish side of the structure; there was a vertical wagon lift on the side of the viaduct down to Calstock Quay, with the old ECMR inclined plane being abandoned.

There were numerous quays all along the River Tamar and a large number of lime kilns. However, over the years, with the virtual eradication of mining in Cornwall and changes in agricultural practice, reliance on coal for fuel diminished, resulting in the virtual disappearance of commercial shipping on the river. The Callington branch line, which opened in 1908 but was cut back to Gunnislake in November 1966, was late to arrive on the scene, by which time potential freight traffic had decreased in volume. The architectural highlight on the steeply graded line is the 120-foot-high Calstock Viaduct, seen here in April 1995 with a two-car Class 150 diesel unit crossing its 12 graceful arches, at SX 434686. *Author*

The new Callington branch opened on 2 March 1908 and was immediately successful, carrying 112,000 passengers in 1913. However, the era of the mines, quarries and brickworks in the area was almost at an end and little use was made of Calstock Quay. The wagon lift attendant was withdrawn and the entire structure was demolished in October 1934. This effectively marked the end of Calstock Quay as a freight-handling location. Freight was withdrawn from the branch line at the beginning of 1966 and although the Callington branch was cut back to Gunnislake in November 1966 the branch line through Calstock is still open and well worth a visit.

Irrespective of railway development in the area, Calstock has been the destination of vessels sailing up from Plymouth for many years and the village remains the focus of summer sailing excursions. However, well over a century has passed since the great days at Calstock Quay.

Falmouth

In the reign of King Henry VIII two castles were built either side of Carrick Roads, at Pendennis and St Mawes. A small settlement existed where the present town of Falmouth is situated and this gradually grew in size, being blessed with a natural deep-water inlet,

Approximately 100 years separate these two photographs of Falmouth Docks. In this Edwardian view dry docks are occupied by sailing and steam ships, the latter being the SS *Alleghany*. Having obtained its charter from King Charles II in 1661, Falmouth enjoyed being the second busiest port in the British Empire for 200 years, due in part to its status as a Royal Mail Packet Station from 1688 to 1852. The deep-water harbour had many quays but the docks as we know them today were built from 1860. *Author's collection*

which developed into a harbour. In 1661 the town received its charter and by 1688 it became a Royal Mail Packet Station. As a result ships travelling all over the discovered world started to use the port, which became the second busiest in the whole of the British Empire. Ships would also call in for 'orders' in those far-off days of primitive communications.

Fishing was an important and developing industry, and in 1790 Fish Strand Quay was constructed. St Anthony's lighthouse was built in 1835 in a strategic position on the eastern side of Carrick Roads, opposite Falmouth. However, there was bad news looming for the town when it lost the Packet Station status in 1852. There followed a series of ups and downs until a group of influential businessmen chaired by Alfred Fox of the famous local family met in 1858 to discuss a plan to build and develop docks at Falmouth, including dry docks, slips, wharfage and storage buildings. The major project would cost an estimated £250,000. The Right Honourable Viscount Falmouth laid a foundation stone in 1860 and the new docks were soon operational. A profit was made immediately, just a few hundred pounds in 1861 but £2,466 by 1863. In addition, the railway from Truro reached the town in 1863, and really opened the doors to an embryo tourist industry, which was to become so important in later years. A number of contracts were won, including the importation of guano (used as fertiliser) from Peru.

In 1870 the Falmouth Harbour Commissioners was formed; this body levied the port dues, policed the port and even dealt with complaints of bullying or assault by seamen. The Commissioners are still at work and collect quite substantial fees from ship-owners in respect of mooring dues and for pilot services. The port suffered a setback when mineral railway lines opened to Fowey in 1869 and 1874, whereas Falmouth had been hoping to develop mineral traffic from the mines and china clay pits. On the other hand, there was growing activity in the ship repair business, resulting in a profit in 1876 of £5,266. However, there were dark clouds looming as iron ships increased in number and repairs to the hundreds of small wooden ships gradually declined. Nevertheless, during the next century Falmouth Docks consolidated its position and, while the docks remained busy and ship repairs continued, the installation never fulfilled its true potential. The docks had an important role during the two World Wars, facilitated by their capability of handling large ocean-going ships.

Efforts were made to regenerate the docks, and in 1958 HRH The Duke of Edinburgh opened the new and very large Queen Elizabeth dry dock. Attempts were also made to find sources of rail traffic to and from the docks, and while there was some container activity, short-term fish trains and even loads of calcified seaweed, none produced long-term income for the docks. Large ships continue to be repaired at Falmouth dry dock and some ship-breaking is undertaken; indeed, the cruise liner and ship repair business is said to be booming. However, in 2002 a report stated that a colossal £80 million needed to be spent to modernise the docks, which in part were 'in an advanced state of disrepair'.

Far removed from small 50-ton wooden fishing smacks at minor Cornish ports in the early 19th century is this 2007 scene of Falmouth Docks, viewed from the same vantage point as the previous photograph. The substantial and apparently booming ship repair facilities at Falmouth can accommodate quite large vessels in four dry docks, such as this P&O Ro-Ro ferry. Falmouth is Cornwall's principal port, but at least in recent years has failed to generate significant volumes of freight traffic. *Author*

Since then a number of ideas have been generated to raise income. In 2007 it was agreed that a large modern state-of-the-art marina would be built at Falmouth with 300 berths at five pontoons and 300 car-parking spaces. There would be a floating breakwater that would afford the marina protection and provide a hook-up for super-yachts and commercial vessels. Another idea was for a shipwreck to be artificially created at Gerrans Bay, near Falmouth, to promote the growing leisure activity of diving. Falmouth is Cornwall's largest port and its place in the county's maritime history is assured, but its early potential was never fully exploited.

Pentewan

The harbour at Pentewan is a very special place to visit in that it is possible, while walking around the old water-filled basin, to half imagine what life must have been like a century and a half ago. The vision of old wooden sailing ships negotiating the narrow dredged sandy channel up past the breakwater to the old and extant lock gates requires only a modicum of clairvoyance. Also there are sufficient remains to envisage the old Pentewan Railway running onto the quay and taking to the elevated section of line in order to discharge loads of china clay. A short section of narrow-gauge track that served a later sand and concrete company adds considerable atmosphere to the scene. In the summer months it is even possible to enjoy a pint at a picnic table on the old north quay opposite the Ship Inn, a St Austell Brewery pub.

Pentewan is a rather special place in terms of its origins, operation and destiny. Sir Christopher Hawkins, the head of another powerful and influential land-owning Cornish family, developed the small harbour of Pentewan for shipping ores and china clay. In 1829 a narrow-gauge railway was built from St Austell for the conveyance of minerals from the mines and pits. Initially horse-operated, steam locomotives were employed from 1873/4. A curious locomotive purchased in 1912 was 2-6-2T *Pioneer*, seen nearing Pentewan on 14 August that year, just five years before the line closed forever. *Author's collection*

This wonderful photograph from the days of sail finds five vessels of the period in the Pentewan Harbour basin. Narrow-gauge sidings can be seen on the left, while on the right is an elevated section of track used by trains that tipped their loads of china clay into the chutes just visible, which discharged directly into the hulls of ships. The water level in the basin was controlled by lock gates, but the harbour regularly experienced severe silting. The last vessel called during 1940 but traffic had been very thin for many years. *Author's collection*

Pentewan, at the mouth of the St Austell river, had been associated with small-scale fishing activities for many years, but in 1744 a basin was built to accommodate a growing number of fishing boats. However, the scale of fishing operations was tiny when compared with nearby Mevagissey, which in 1850 supported about 50 fishing vessels. The small harbour and the surrounding area was owned by the Hawkins family, who also had extensive mining interests, including Cornwall's largest lead mine at East Wheal Rose. Sir Christopher Hawkins and his family also owned china clay pits and, with the advent of the burgeoning mineral extraction business, they logically proposed to further develop Pentewan, especially as they had seen the profitable nearby port of Charlestown blossom following development by the Rashleigh family.

In 1818 Hawkins granted a 60-year lease to one John Stanley, acting on behalf of the Pentewan Harbour Company. Shortly after the signing, work started on deepening the basin, providing new quays and lock gates and building a protective pier. The new harbour was ready for use in 1820 but the works had cost five times the original estimate. The usage figures were rather low to start with. In April 1824, for example, only two ships used the harbour, and a further two in June, but this had increased to 13 by July. Even though there was 1,132 feet of wharfage at Pentewan, with 26-foot-wide lock gates, the visiting ships were small, averaging about 65 tons each. It became clear to Hawkins that if Pentewan was to become a great success it would require rail access. He also developed the area around the harbour, and between 1826 and 1851 the village

Although all of the buildings on the east quay have since been modified in some way they can still be identified a century after the previous photograph was taken. All the ships have long gone but the scene is pleasant and tranquil and it is still possible to explore the derelict lock gates in the right background. Where ships were once loaded picnic tables provide open-air seating for drinkers at the adjacent Ship Inn public house (SX 019472). *Author*

grew from 29 to 71 dwellings with the population rising to 350. Hawkins tried to raise the finance for construction but was obliged to 'go it alone', thereby running up substantial debts. Unfortunately he died in 1829, aged 71, and never saw the railway finished. The estate was taken over by the nine-year-old Christopher (Henry Thomas) Hawkins, who was to own the railway and harbour for the next 74 years!

In its earliest days Pentewan was a small-scale fishing port and, indeed, as early as 1819 fish cellars were located by the old pier. In 1885 24,960 tons of china clay were exported from the harbour, the fourth busiest port after Fowey, Par and Charlestown. About the turn of the 20th century a number of excursions were run from St Austell with members of the public travelling in china clay wagons for a day's outing at Pentewan (see page 152). One of the harbour's many problems was its inability to receive ships of more than about 200 tons. With weeds growing in the choked harbour entrance behind the old lock gates, this was the scene in 2002. *Author*

Although there had for years been activity in the sand, gravel and concrete business on the south side of Pentewan Harbour, between the early 1950s and 1965 there was a 2ft 6in-gauge railway serving the works and extending onto the pier. A small engine shed was located by the abandoned lock gates, and the remains are seen here in September 2002. Note the sand-blocked access channel on the left, and Mevagissey Bay beyond. *Author*

The narrow-gauge horse-worked Pentewan Railway opened in 1829, but it was 1830 before it was completed in all respects, at a total cost of £5,732. Initially business was hardly brisk, with only 86 ships using the harbour in 1830 and 72 in 1831, only one or two per working week. However, there was a substantial upturn in business during the next few years and unbelievably Pentewan was to become the third busiest port in Cornwall, based on china clay shipments only. Unfortunately one of the Pentewan Railway's main customers got into financial difficulty in 1833 and by 1838 only one-tenth of Cornwall's total china clay (and china stone) output was exported through the little harbour. There were other loads hauled on the Pentewan such as inbound coal and limestone, but traffic was extremely volatile and over a 14-year period between 1829 and 1843 an average profit of only £91 per year was returned, with a loss being incurred in some years.

Pentewan Harbour was perpetually under a two-pronged attack that affected smooth operations. On the land side the St Austell River carried tons of mine waste down from the mines and pits and, although there were reservoirs above the harbour, some of this waste spilled into the main basin. However, by far the most serious problem was the continuous silting of the harbour, as the waves deposited huge volumes of sand onto the beach that formed the entry channel to the basin. Within a short period of time huge sand dunes would build up, preventing shipping from entering. Captains were obviously keen to avoid running aground or damaging the hulls of their ships, resulting in Pentewan becoming an unpopular maritime location. The main access channel to the harbour was frequently dredged, but following every storm, with the inevitable heavy seas, more dredging would be necessary. This all had an impact on costs but, worse still, caused delays to the ships. This created a psychological barrier where ships' Masters became less enthusiastic about risking a visit to Pentewan. During a visit by the good ship *Merton* the crew had to dump good coal into the sea to lighten their ship before access could be gained.

In 1843 Hawkins leased the harbour and railway to a group of mine-owners and landowners who formed the Pentewan Harbour & Railway Company. For the next 30 years the fortunes of the Pentewan prospered and in 1872, prior to the formation of the rival Cornwall Minerals Railway, Par shipped 52,000 tons of china clay, Charlestown 36,000 tons and Pentewan 20,000 tons. The railway was relaid to a 2ft 6in gauge and steam locomotives were used on the line for the first time. However, this work, combined with a monster sand bar, resulted in virtual closure for Pentewan. Moreover, in 1873/4 there was downturn in the china clay industry. Nevertheless, phoenix-like, the operation recovered and by 1889 a record 45,270 tons was carried on the railway. However, from that date there was a terminal decline in the fortunes of Pentewan, and by 1904 only 2% of all the china clay produced in Cornwall was shipped from there.

By 1900 all of the lime kilns had closed, but on the bright side a 189-ton ship entered the harbour in 1908. In 1909 a stone breakwater was constructed, which extended 260 feet beyond the pier, and in 1911 continuing problems with silting saw a crane permanently employed to keep the channel clear. Nevertheless traffic slowly dwindled and a prolonged strike by clay workers in 1913 and the onset of the First World War a year later were disastrous. In 1915 only 90 vessels entered Pentewan, in 1916 it was 51 and in 1917 only 34. The last load on the railway was carried in 1918, whereupon the line closed and was lifted shortly afterwards. One of the problems with the railway was that it never reached the china clay pits and clay had to be transhipped from carts to railway wagons at St Austell. A last load of china clay arrived by road in 1929, which was loaded into the ship *Duchess*. A sand and concrete company flourished and small vessels continued to use the harbour sporadically until 1940, but the harbour then silted up and would never see shipping again. The sand and concrete business continued until February 1965 but the only signs of life are now seabirds and visitors, although the village is still vibrant, especially in the summer months.

Hayle

Hayle is yet another Cornish port with a history going back to Roman times, and it is known that the Romans mined, or at least streamed, tin just 4 miles from the estuary of the Hayle River. In common with other Cornish ports, it was the growth of tin mining, closely followed by copper, that initiated the development at Hayle, with two tin-smelting houses being established there between 1710 and 1720. One of the few copper smelters in Cornwall was at Copperhouse, just to the east of the main harbour area; it was served by a short canal built by John Edwards. Smelting ceased in 1806 because it was far more economic to convey the ore to South Wales for smelting than to bring huge volumes of coal from South Wales to Cornwall. The large smelter building continued in business as a foundry until the mining crash of the mid-1860s, when it was taken over by the Harvey Company.

Harveys of Hayle was founded by John Harvey, a blacksmith who built a forge beside the waters of the estuary. The business grew and without doubt his company had an enormous influence in the development of Hayle. Harvey's timing was perfection, as by 1750 it is said that about 600 horses and mules laden with ore or coal were traipsing daily between the mining areas around Camborne, Carn Brea and Redruth and the harbour at Hayle. The forge quickly developed into a foundry and within a few years there seemed no limit to Harveys' product line, which ranged from large steam engines to miscellaneous mining equipment and, after the mid-1860s, large iron ocean-going ships. The foundry grew quickly, so that at its peak the company employed 1,000 local people. In 1819 Harveys built a new 450-yard wharf and a number of permanent quays at Carnsew and along Penpol Creek at Hayle, dredging and deepening the harbour area.

Hayle town also grew, and soon boasted all of the amenities associated with a community of its size. Two major milestones occurred, the first in about 1831 when

In terms of industry and transport the Hayle of today is, compared with its heyday, a rather sad place. The great foundries have gone, the explosives factories have closed, the power station has been demolished, commercial shipping has ceased using the port, quayside buildings have been razed to the ground, there are no buildings on the station platforms and large-scale redevelopment has not occurred on any significant scale. By contrast, in 1904 two colliers including the SS *Hayle* are unloaded at the quayside and railway wagons line the quay. *Author's collection*

steamer services commenced between Hayle and Bristol (from 1841 passengers could travel onward by rail from Bristol to London). The second was in 1834 when proposals to build a railway from Hayle to the mining areas received Royal Assent; the Act was amended in 1836. In December 1837 the Hayle Railway opened its line from Hayle to Portreath, and the following year to Tresavean Mine and Redruth. The line included a number of inclines, but otherwise steam locomotives were used to convey the ores, coals and timber between harbour and mine. Passengers were carried from 1841. In 1843 there were two passenger trains per day and this had increased to three by July 1844. The Hayle Railway was taken over by the West Cornwall Railway in 1846, and in 1852

Some fine old terraces that were once the homes of foundry workers remain at Hayle. In 1758 the Cornish Copper Company established a foundry on Copperhouse Creek and Harveys followed in 1779. In 1875 Harveys acquired the Cornish Copper Company, but by then the peak of Cornwall's mining activity had passed. Harveys was famous for its beam engines and later for shipbuilding, but other forms of steam propulsion could be found in the streets of Hayle, such as this crane traction engine and three stout wagons, seen in early Edwardian times. *Cornish Studies Library*

125

This view shows the Hayle of old, with steamers and sailing ships aplenty at the wharves, railway wagons everywhere, industrial buildings in use, piles of coal on the quays and even a traction engine posing for the camera. A power station was established in 1910, but it closed in 1977 and its chimneys were subsequently blown up. However, the railway viaduct in the far distance is still in use! *Author's collection*

its new main line between Redruth and Penzance opened, avoiding the inclines (retained on the branches) and crossing the town of Hayle on a 277-yard-long curved viaduct.

The West Cornwall Railway was linked with the Cornwall Railway at Truro from 1859 but through running from London to Penzance was only possible from 1867 when dual-gauge track was completed. By 1883 it was possible to travel from Hayle to London in about 9 hours; in 1790 a coach from Exeter to Falmouth took 21 hours! The entire network was converted to standard gauge in 1892. From 1852 a steeply graded spur from the main line to the harbour was provided. Leaving the main line just east of the viaduct at the western end of Hayle station, the 55-chain branch descended at 1 in 30. There was also a 25-chain siding along the north side of the old Copperhouse Creek to Sandhills, used for years by traffic to and from an explosives factory. Broad-gauge tracks were added in 1877. A signal box controlled the entrance to the wharves rail complex.

Most of wharves were served by rail; indeed, to reach the quays on the western side of the harbour the old Hayle Railway lines in front of Penpol Terrace were used, which then curved in a wide 'U' shape under the main-line viaduct. Wagons were always horse-drawn on this section. A coal-fired power station was built at Hayle to provide power for the town and its many industrial installations, and colliers lined rail-served quays all along the eastern side of the harbour. Another siding served the local gasworks and later an oil storage depot, at the north end of the complex. To give an idea of the scale of operations, there was siding provision for up to 300 general goods wagons and 50 oil

The Hayle Railway opened its line to Redruth in stages from 1837, long before the Cornwall Railway opened the Royal Albert Bridge. A new main-line alignment from Truro to Penzance opened in 1852 and a steeply graded branch from this had to be constructed down to the wharves, with a short section at 1 in 30. In the harbour area there was a remarkable network of railway lines. In this delightful view, taken on 4 July 1960, 0-6-0 pannier tank No 9748 propels its 'Toad' brake-van down to the wharves to indulge in a little shunting. Note the power station chimneys on the right. *J. C. Beckett*

This view shows the depressing scene of total dereliction on Hayle wharves in September 2002. The old railway lines are still visible and a single building has defied the demolition men. The scene was similar five years later, with just an old dredger tied up at the quay with a few lobster-pots in storage. John Harvey and Richard Trevithick would no doubt turn in their graves at such a sight. *Author*

tank wagons. The line was normally worked by small 0-6-0 or 2-6-2 steam tank locomotives, and in later years Class 22 and 25 diesels.

After more than a century of growth the Cornish mining industry was coming to an end. The industry had struggled on for decades but as the mines got deeper they became more expensive to operate and cheap imports from foreign countries made Cornish mining non-viable. It had all but finished by 1900 and in 1904 the unthinkable happened when Harveys' foundry closed its doors. For some decades the harbour continued to see some general and power station traffic, but Hayle Harbour was difficult to operate and frequent dredging became necessary if larger ships were to continue to call. Hayle lifeboat station closed in 1920, a sure indicator of decline. A large number of the minor ancillary industries also gradually closed. A sprinkling of commercial vessels continued to call, but during the 1970s it was announced that the power station would close and that the oil depot would no longer be rail-served. The last train down the historic little branch line ran in January 1981.

Although there is a pleasant walk along the north side of Copperhouse Pool, much of the harbour and wharves are now derelict, part of the South Quay recently collapsed, and there is hardly any income for the Harbour Commissioners to effect repairs. For the past nine years development companies, councils and government agencies have been in discussion and it has been suggested that £100 million is required for redevelopment; a 36-acre harbour with a permanent water depth, a marina and 400 houses have been proposed, but the finance has simply not been forthcoming.

Trevaunance

The port of Trevaunance should perhaps have been called St Agnes Harbour, so near was it to the town. There was an important mining area around St Agnes, including Wheal Ellen, Wheal Coates, Wheal Kitty and Cligga Head, and as ever the transport of minerals for shipment was all-important. It was also hoped that Trevaunance would provide a north coast port for Truro, some 8 miles distant. Although near Truro, the location chosen for this small harbour was particularly vulnerable to rough seas and was unique in being constructed and partially constructed five times, only to be totally destroyed by the sea on every occasion.

If ever there was a story to demonstrate the power of the sea, it is man's attempt to build a harbour at Trevaunance at St Agnes. The first attempt to build a harbour was in 1632 (destroyed 1633), the second in 1684 (destroyed 1684), the third in 1699 (destroyed 1705), the fourth in 1710 (destroyed 1736), and the fifth in 1794 (destroyed after 1910). The last-built proved to be of only limited use during the peak mining years in the 19th century, due to its compact size. A tramway carried ore to the harbour and there was some remarkable and complex wooden staging (visible top left) for loading vessels.
Cornish Studies Library

The Cornish north coast is rugged and finding a suitable location to build a harbour was always difficult. None of the small ports eventually built along the coast were without problems. Between St Ives and Bude (inclusive) there were 19 locations that ships regularly visited or where they were beached. All were small ports and many had extremely difficult entrances, such as Boscastle, Portreath and Padstow, the latter with its infamous Doom Bar. Throughout the Middle Ages loads of coal, timber, charcoal and general goods were conveyed in small barques, smacks and brigs that crossed the Bristol Channel with goods bound for Truro. They were often beached on the River Gannel estuary near Newquay or on the sands at Perranporth. The first thoughts about providing a harbour nearer to Truro are attributed to John Tonkin. In 1632 the Tonkin family invested much money in providing a new pier, or quay, but the following winter a devastating storm smashed all that had been achieved and it would be many years before a further attempt was made.

In 1684 family successor Hugh Tonkin tried for a second time to establish a small port. He chose a slightly different location and spent several hundred pounds cutting away part of a cliff and securing rocks, but such was the violence of the sea that all that had been achieved over several months of hard manual effort was destroyed in a storm. On the next two occasions the family employed a famous designer, Henry Winstanley, to design a strongly built harbour. This was duly done and all appeared to be well until, during a severe summer storm in August 1705, the structures were simply swept away. Hugh subsequently died and his son Thomas Tonkin was determined to build the harbour that his ancestors had craved. In 1710 he spent £6,000, an absolute fortune in those days, using great granite blocks laid in hot lime brought from Aberthaw in South Wales, which would set as hard as the rock itself. The harbour was completed but a protective breakwater was never built as the family fortunes had dissipated. Apparently a small breach occurred during a severe storm and there were insufficient funds to repair it. The breach widened, then in 1736 a gale whipping up mountainous seas obliterated Trevaunance Harbour from the map.

By the end of the 18th century the great mining boom years were commencing and there was a genuine need in the area for an artificial harbour, so in 1793 a group of entrepreneurs prepared an Act of Parliament for the construction of a new one. The immediate topography prevented the envisaged harbour from being anything but small, but approval was given and by 1794 the sum of £10,000 had been raised. The new and fifth harbour was at the foot of the cliffs, and above the quays there was wooden loading apparatus that looked decidedly 'Heath Robinson'. Although only a few ships could use the harbour at any one time, it was successful for more than a century, handling outbound ores but particularly inbound coal, mainly from South Wales. These loads were hauled up the cliff by horse-worked winding gear. A handful of ships were built in the vicinity.

The harbour was something of a curiosity, but in 1910 the structure yet again succumbed to the power of the sea. Now just a pile of rocks remain, but they make a fascinating sight from the footpath above the sandy and rocky cove, with a few surrounding engine houses standing as the silent sentinels of times past.

One of the most remarkable sights in Cornwall are the present-day remains of Trevaunance Harbour. As can be seen in this April 2007 scene the harbour has been flattened by the sea and now comprises simply a pile of granite blocks just above sea level. All of the mines closed and the complex wooden staging crumbled more than a century ago. A walk along the cliffs here, at SW 720518, is recommended. *Author*

Roads

There are many wonderful old medieval road bridges in Cornwall: the 14th-century bridge at Wadebridge, the 1412 Treverbyn Bridge, the 1520 Respryn Bridge and the Tudor bridge at Lostwithiel are just a few examples of survivors. Also of note are the surviving and ancient moorland 'clapper' bridges, which comprise long slabs of granite located on stone supports. There are many reports of road journeys into Cornwall in the Middle Ages and such roads as existed were merely tracks with ruts and potholes aplenty. Most travel was either on horseback or on foot, and all goods continued to be carried by pack animals, quite often with sacks simply being slung over their backs. A dray or sledge was sometimes used, but it would be 1750 before a dray was fitted with wheels and 1790 before wagons of any description were used. Some of the aristocratic families had coaches in the mid-18th century, which were used primarily on their estates, one of the first being the Hawkins family of

It is now hard to imagine the situation that prevailed prior to 1760, when the Turnpike Trusts were created. There were no metalled roads as we know them, just crude tracks that became almost impassable during the wet winter months. In the summer dust replaced mud, and above all else any journey of substance took a remarkable amount of time to complete. Some of the earliest 'road' structures, where tracks had to cross rivers and streams, were 'clapper' bridges, comprising granite slabs laid longitudinally across stone supports, as seen in this ancient example at Bradford (SX 119754) on the edge of Bodmin Moor. *Author*

Trewinnard, near St Erth. By the end of the century the increasing use of wheeled vehicles was made possible only by Turnpike Trusts, 14 of which were established in Cornwall by Act of Parliament between 1769 and 1849.

The Trusts were effectively businesses whereby often primitive roads were improved and graded and users would pay very high tolls at strategically placed toll gates to travel

Throughout Cornwall there are some impressive and attractive medieval bridges, a good example being Respryn Bridge (SX 098635) over the River Fowey, to the west of Bodmin Parkway station. Another ancient gem, also crossing the River Fowey, can be found at Lostwithiel (SX 105598), photographed here in September 2007. The railway station is immediately to the right of this scene. *Author*

along them. Some of the turnpikes were major undertakings such as that between Torpoint and Truro, which had several cuttings through solid rock and more declivities than any other in Cornwall. Among the earliest turnpikes were Truro-Falmouth, Truro-Grampound, Launceston-Wadebridge via Camelford, Truro-Penzance, Torpoint-Truro via Liskeard, Lostwithiel, St Blazey and St Austell, Launceston-Truro via Bodmin (the origins of the main A30 road), and Penryn-Helston.

Until the 18th century most goods were conveyed by pack animals, with wagons not making an appearance until the end of the century. The first recorded coach in Cornwall was in 1644. Once the Turnpike Trusts were established road improvements followed, with travellers normally paying a toll to use the relevant section of road. The building of these roads broadly coincided with the provision of stage and mail coaches in Cornwall, which carried passengers, mail and packages from town to town. Here the 'Brilliant' horse omnibus service passes Old Ponsandane House, home of the Bolitho family, near Penzance in 1843. It connected with the railway to Redruth and the steamer to Bristol at Hayle. *Courtesy of Penzance Corporation*

In 1814 stagecoaches were well established and the four primary routes were Launceston-Truro, Truro-Falmouth, Truro-Penzance and Torpoint-Truro. For many years there was competition between coach operators, and 'racing' accidents were not unknown. The mail coach routes were quite good for the period but the side roads were not much travelled. However, the Turnpike Acts had succeeded in establishing a network of roads between principal Cornish towns, especially between 1820 and 1849. Increasing prosperity and a booming mining industry, combined with a rapidly growing population and a desire to trade, created a demand for better roads and by now Cornwall's roads were, at least in summer, no longer as notorious and could be compared favourably with those of other counties.

Travel by coach and horse omnibuses continued into the Edwardian era, considerably outliving the Turnpike Trusts, which had all expired by 1873. By then the internal

This wonderful structure is on the road from St Breward to Blisland, where it crosses the De Lank River. As can be seen from the massive granite slabs, Delford Clapper Bridge (SX 114759) was built on conventional lines, but as late as the 1890s. *Author*

Right: In the latter part of the 18th century it took the best part of a week to travel from Falmouth to London and the cost was extortionate by today's standards. Gradually competition and improving roads brought down journey times and costs, and by the 1850s coaches ran from Penzance to Plymouth, to connect with the train that overall offered a journey to London in a single day! Gradually roads improved and the coming of the railways and the arrival of the motor car ousted the horse-drawn coaches, the last of which ran in the Bude area in 1919. The main road into Cornwall has always been the A30 and this view shows the first and last signpost in England, at Land's End. *Author's collection*

Below: Gradually metalled roads covered the whole of the county, and over the decades, as traffic volumes increased, particularly in the summer months, road improvements have continued apace. Many of the Cornish lanes remain unchanged but new major arteries have thankfully been constructed, with much-needed improvements on the A30 at Goss Moor and on the A38 at Dobwalls being the latest upgrades. Many travellers were thankful for the early completion in July 2007 of this stretch of dual carriageway on the A30 near Roche, which avoided the dreaded Goss Moor single-carriageway stretch. *Author*

combustion engine was making its presence felt both in terms of personal transport and commercial vehicles. By 1903 motorbuses were in operation and eventually all but the most minor of roads were metalled. Over the years the surface of roads improved, especially with the widespread use of tarmacadam. Important roads were all given either 'A' or 'B' numbers and these designations survive today. During the past 60 years the only major problem has been improving roads in an attempt to accommodate the explosion in private car ownership. This endless but necessary process has most recently been evident in works on the A30 across Goss Moor and the A38 at Dobwalls, earlier bypasses such as Bodmin, Liskeard, Penzance and Hayle having been great successes.

Horse power

Horses have been a part of the Cornish transport scene for as long as humans have occupied the land. For centuries the only way to travel substantial distances was on horseback, and wheeled vehicular traffic was unknown. Horses were extremely versatile and, whether used

For centuries the horse was the primary means of transport in Cornwall. Whether singly for individuals, as a team for coach travel or in line for freight wagon haulage, their versatility was exploited. In many instances horses were provided by families specialising in their provision, such as the Hoytes family of Newquay, which owned large numbers of horses that were contracted to haul wagons on tramways or local stagecoaches. In this wonderful Edwardian scene at Newquay, before such vehicles were replaced by the motor buses, this North Cornwall Coach Company vehicle is full to the brim with a Wadebridge working. *Newquay Old Cornwall Society*

as personal transport, in agriculture, as pack animals or even down the mines, their contribution was invaluable. One of the most interesting uses was with the British Post Office, which was established in 1644. A notice in the *London Gazette* in October 1668 gave notice that a new horse post would carry letters between Exeter and 'Launston' (Launceston) twice every week. The network was greatly extended but horses ruled the roost for more than a century before mail coaches appeared in Cornwall from 1785. Even after that date horses continued to be used, a letter from London to Penzance taking three days in 1808.

The earliest use of horse power was in the world of agriculture. In addition to conventional ploughing, horses operated a wide range of farm equipment in an age that substantially pre-dated either the steam or internal combustion engine. Once wagons and other farm vehicles were in general use there was scarcely a farm that could ignore horse power. By the 18th century horses and mules were used in their thousands as pack animals conveying all manner of commodities between the mines and pits and the ports and beaches. Loads were either placed in panniers or strapped across the backs of the beasts, which were often led in tethered teams. Once wagons started to appear in some number there were various configurations employed. Small two-wheeled carts were mostly handled by a single horse, but a 3-ton wagon full of china clay would often require a team of three horses, especially if gradients were involved.

This stunning view for equestrian enthusiasts was taken at Camborne railway station in Victorian times. There is almost a traffic jam as various types of horse-drawn vehicle, including the mail coach, await the arrival of the London train in the station's approach, which was inconveniently located on the up side. The brick building survives today, as does the replacement 1940 overbridge, but the awnings and the signal box have long gone. *Cornish Studies Library*

Horses were not only used on journeys between mines and ports but also within individual mines and pits. In some of the larger mines horses were used underground, hauling small tippler-type tramway wagons from the face of the lode to the loading mechanism or crushers. On the surface in particular, horses often worked in teams, hauling rakes of several wagons weighing in total 50 tons or more from one part of an installation to another. On the very first long-distance tramway, the Poldice Tramway of 1812, which ran down to the harbour at Portreath, all wagons were horse-drawn and this situation also prevailed on the Treffry Tramways from 1841 until 1873, the Redruth & Chasewater Railway from 1825 until 1854, and the Pentewan Railway between 1829 and 1873. Prior to the widespread use of the steam engine in mines, horses were used on whims, where they walked around a capstan either lifting or lowering a load in a mine shaft. Another industrial use for horses was in shunting railway wagons. For example, on the wharves of Hayle Harbour horses were used on the Penpol Terrace line well into the 1960s, under the auspices of British Railways. In earlier years the lines on the quay at Newquay were horse-shunted and wagons were hauled through the streets of the town until 1922. In some of these instances the provision of horses was subcontracted to specialist companies such as Hoytes of Newquay. Horses were also used for wagon haulage at Fowey Docks and many other locations.

This poor old nag is standing in the harbour at St Ives with a small single-axle wagon while fish are loaded from a tiny fishing vessel. The ensemble will later make its way up the slip and into the town. Dozens of seagulls can be seen in the background waiting in hope for a gratuitous meal. The postcard was posted in 1934 and although the photograph is obviously earlier it does demonstrate the continuing use of horses up to and beyond World War 2. *Author's collection*

Horse power was not only used on the roads and in the mines but on tramways and railways, and many of the early mineral lines relied on horses to haul wagons over quite significant distances. The last known location where horses powered railway wagons was on Hayle Wharves, an activity that surprisingly lasted into the 1960s.

Locomotives were banned from the line, which ran towards the old Harveys foundry along Penpol Terrace. With plenty of wagons in the background, a 'double-headed' working is about to move a loaded wagon (see the section on Hayle). *Author's collection*

Many small businesses engaged in everything from home deliveries, especially milk, bread and coal, to collecting fish from the local harbour used horses and carts of various dimensions. Brewers' drays also helped provide manure for the local community! Horses and carriages were commonly used in the 19th century to convey the gentry, to transfer railway passengers from station to hotel, and as the Victorian equivalent of taxis. Nowadays the expression 'coach and horses' normally refers to a public house, but from the late 18th century horse-drawn stagecoaches were used increasingly throughout Cornwall, and continued to be for just over a century. In some of the larger towns there was also a brief period when horse-drawn omnibuses could be seen, powered by a team of two, four or even six horses. There were many other applications not mentioned, but the contribution of our four-legged friends cannot be underestimated.

Traction engines

The history of the traction engine is particularly relevant to Cornwall in that it was Richard Trevithick who invented and built the first mobile British steam-powered vehicle in 1801 when he was living in the county. He also built several steam road carriages. Stationary steam engines were in agricultural use in the mid-1800s but they were not self-propelling and had to be hauled around farms by horses. Many of these engines were simply portable

Traction engines, steamrollers and steam-powered agricultural machinery all played their part in the development of industrial and transport history in Cornwall. Indeed, it was Richard Trevithick who invented a high-pressure steam engine, a road locomotive and the world's first successful steam locomotive. Sometimes accidents happened, even in the best regulated of circles, and on 29 March 1905 the driver of this Fowler traction engine, *Imperatrix*, has lost control in Fore Street, Marazion, demolishing a stone wall and falling down an embankment. As ever a crowd has congregated for the photographer. *Cornish Studies Library*

steam power plants used in a variety of applications. There were also specific steam ploughing engines that usually worked in pairs, on either side of a particular field.

The first traction engines as we now know them were produced about 1840, and a number of British firms such as Ransome, Aveling, Burrell, Clayton, Fowler and Garrett became associated with their manufacture. The heyday of the steam road-going traction engine was from 1880 until about 1920, when they were in demand as road locomotives, used for heavy haulage on public roads. Other 'traction engines' included steam tractors, which were smaller versions of the locomotives, showman's engines used at fairs and circuses, and steamrollers that were used in road building until the 1960s.

In general terms traction engines were slow-moving and they had limited manoeuvrability. The larger ones were immensely powerful and could haul trailing loads of up to 120 tons. The steam roadrollers could turn the scales at 30 tons but once tarmac was introduced it was found that the optimum weight was half that figure. There were of course other types of steam propulsion ranging from a handful of early automobiles to the steam lorry. Foden and Sentinel were two of the protagonists, but by about 1930 the flexibility offered by internal-combustion-engined lorries was irresistible to operators and steam lorries gradually disappeared.

Street trams

Although Cornwall was riddled with industrial installations that employed many weird and wonderful devices to move materials about the works, mine or pit, there was only ever one street tramway system in the whole of the county. In 1898, towards the end of Queen Victoria's reign, an efficient public transport system was proposed between the heavily populated mining towns of Redruth and Camborne; in 1901 the population of Redruth was 10,451 and Camborne 14,726. Successful electric street tramway systems had been working elsewhere in the UK and, before the age of the motor bus, a similar

Cornwall was not noted for its street tramways and west of Plymouth the only system of note was the Camborne & Redruth Tramway of the Urban Electric Supply Co Ltd. In this delightful bromesko photograph of 1901 the intensity of the manual labour involved in the building of the line is remarkable. Here a local road is being excavated for the 3ft 6in trackbed, literally a 'picks and shovels' job. *Cornish Studies Library*

system with proven technology was the preferred option in this part of Cornwall. Construction of the Camborne & Redruth Tramway, a subsidiary of the Urban Electric Supply Co Ltd, got under way in 1901/2 and the line, 3 miles 32 chains long, opened on 7 November 1902. As the photographs show, the building of the tramway was a colossal manual task utilising the minimum amount of machinery. A proposed 5-mile extension from Redruth to Portreath was never built.

The company acquired a fleet of eight four-wheeled tramcars, six double-deckers with open tops and two single-deck cars. All the cars were manufactured by C. F. Milnes with two 28hp electric motors, and all carried a striking dark green and cream livery. They had reversible seats so that passengers could choose which way they wanted to face (normally forward). The double-deck cars were numbered 1-4 and 7 and 8, while the single-deck cars were Nos 5 and 6. The cars were positively festooned with advertisements, including some for the Redruth Brewery Co Ltd, although there are no reports of complaints from the active Temperance movement!

One unusual aspect of the Camborne & Redruth operation was the running of mineral trains from November 1903. Two electric tram locomotives, each with two 25hp motors, were employed on mineral workings from East Pool and Wheal Agar tin and copper mines to the stamps and smelter at Tolvaddon. The ore was conveyed in 14 small side-tipping wagons and contemporary photographs show loads of either three or

Oops! Another accident by another traction engine. The construction of the Camborne & Redruth Tramway did not always go smoothly and this incident would have caused a major problem. While working at East Hill, Tucking Mill, early in 1902 the roadway gave way under the weight of this machine. As in the photograph in the section on Hayle, the engine was hauling trailers loaded with materials at the time. Note the wooden 'props' against the wheels of the engine to prevent it toppling further, and again the usual gathering of onlookers. *Cornish Studies Library*

four wagons comprising a single 'train'. The locomotives were built without cabs, but in the 1920s they were rebuilt with wooden bodies that afforded the crews a modicum of protection from the weather. From September 1904 some of the passenger tramcars carried letters, and special letterboxes were attached to their dashboards. One working per day conveyed mail bags and the relevant cars were known as 'postal cars', which carried large signs displayed on the upper deck.

Right: Much of the tramway was single track but with passing loops. In this 1911 view at Barn Couse loop car No 2 passes car No 3; there were six open-top double-deck trams in the fleet and two single-deck. The length of the tramway was 3 miles 4 chains and it opened to passengers in November 1902 and a year later for local ore trains. The two drivers and one of the conductors are posing for the camera. *Cornish Studies Library*

Above: This wonderfully animated picture would seem to depict a scene from the early days of the tramway. The Edwardian dress is fascinating and very much a part of the social history of the period. Two cars are passing at the bottom of Pool Hill, midway between the two principal towns. The cars were 28 feet long overall and rested on four-wheeled underframes. *Author's collection*

The tramway was unusual in that from November 1903 it transported ore from East Pool and Wheal Agar mines to a smelter at Tolvaddon. For that purpose it possessed two small 25hp electric locomotives and a number of side-tipping freight wagons. Passenger services succumbed to bus competition in 1927 but the ore trains continued until 1934, when an aerial ropeway was introduced. Here a 'freight' prepares to leave East Pool mine surrounded by interesting local animation. *Author's collection*

TRAMMING TIN STONE, EAST POOL MINE, NEAR REDRUTH

Much of the tramway was single track but there were seven passing loops and a short section of double track at Pool; the exact figures were 2 miles 61 chains of single track and 51 chains of double track. There was a separate branch line to Tolvaddon, which, together with short stubs into the actual mines, amounted to 71 chains. The tramway had its own power source at the depot, where there was a boiler house with a stack and electricity generators. In the early days the tramway was very successful, but with the demise of the mining industry and the arrival of motorbuses and motor cars the writing was on the wall at a very early date. After only a quarter of a century of operation the tramway was closed, the last passenger car traversing the route on 29 September 1927. Surprisingly the freight operation continued for a further seven years, but in 1934 it too succumbed, being replaced by an aerial ropeway that conveyed the ore in buckets until the mines closed.

It seems strange in today's 'eco-friendly carbon footprinted' world that the trams should have been taken off quite so soon. Although the old Camborne & Redruth was Cornwall's only street tramway there were other proposals. In 1889 a 1.55-mile standard-gauge street tramway had been proposed and approved between Penzance railway station and the fishing town of Newlyn. However, the plan required a number of houses to be demolished

At the start of the 20th century four rubber tyres began to replace four metal-shod hooves. In the latter category, however, it was hard to beat the pulling power of a pair of oxen, and by the 1920s, when this scene was recorded in Mount Pleasant Road, Camborne, it appears to have already become something of a novelty. This ox cart was owned by a local butcher who is advertising his best beef suet on the side of the vehicle. Whatever the occasion, the children are having a good time! *Cornish Studies Library*

and local pressure saw the scheme abandoned. Ironically a harbour-front road was built on the same alignment.

Although slightly removed from street tramways, in 1911 a scheme was produced for a 3-mile trolleybus system between Falmouth and Penryn. The system was described as 'railless' and the company involved was the 'Railless Electric Traction Co Ltd. The scheme never came to fruition.

Motor transport

In common with the rest of the UK the very first motor cars arrived in Cornwall about 1900. Initially a showpiece for the very wealthy, these early and fairly crude machines were regarded as something of a novelty. There were few creature comforts, few purveyors of fuel, draconian speed limits and questionable reliability. There were many examples of horses and animals being frightened by the sight and the sound of these now veteran vehicles. It was necessary to register all vehicles and eventually a county identification scheme was introduced, with the letters AF, CV and RL all being specific to Cornwall. In the photograph in the Buses section, taken in about 1903 outside Hill's Hotel at the Lizard, we see one of the very first cars in Cornwall, AF 18, and two early GWR Milnes-Daimler buses, AF 66 and AF 84.

The road improvements undertaken by the Turnpike Trusts had put in place a basic network, but only gradually would the main highways be metalled. This allowed traffic to proceed even in wet winter conditions, whereas a few years previously most vehicles would have become bogged down in the ruts and potholes. All but the most minor roads were surfaced, with tarmacadam being used increasingly on a base of ballast. Over the decades road traffic grew considerably in Cornwall, including private cars, vans, commercial vehicles and public service vehicles.

Gradually cars were becoming more affordable and before the Second World War nearly all of the popular car manufacturers, which were mostly based in the UK, were producing small and cheap cars for the middle classes, such as the Austin 7, Morris 8 and Ford 8. British car-makers such as Austin, Morris, Vauxhall, Riley, Wolseley, MG, Sunbeam, Hillman, Rover, Humber, Daimler, Jaguar, Lanchester, Bentley and Rolls-Royce,

The history of the motor car in Cornwall is not greatly different from elsewhere in the UK. From the turn of the 20th century and prior to the First World War there began an increase in car ownership, which started with only the most wealthy and upper-class members of the community. This extended to the middle classes just before and after the Second World War, and from the 1960s and 1970s to the general public at large. The primary association of registration letters with the County of Cornwall was and still is AF, as seen here on this automobile outside Truro station in 1915. Injured soldiers seem to be returning from combat. *Cornish Studies Library*

In this wonderful study at Carbis Bay station on the St Ives branch four ladies are being collected from the station and are about to be taken to their hotel. Their not inconsiderable luggage has been loaded onto a donkey cart, overseen by a uniformed attendant. Note the spindly wheels on the car, the spare tyres on the running board and the YA Somerset registration. The photograph is undated, but would appear to be from the 1920s. *Cornish Studies Library*

became household names. Even the names of the individual models both before and after the Second World War were typically English, such as Dorset, Devon, Cambridge, Oxford, Isis, Westminster, Victor, Imp, Elf, Hunter, Rapier, Sovereign, Super Snipe, Silver Cloud, and so on. This wonderful era would end abruptly as at first the Japanese, then other Far Eastern countries, not to mention post-war European car-makers, invaded what had previously been almost a closed shop.

From the 'never had it so good' era in the 1960s and 1970s, car ownership simply exploded at a time when UK-owned car firms (except for minor specialist manufacturers) became extinct. In the past 40 years Cornwall's population has grown by a staggering 45% and traffic has grown by more than 250%. The population of Cornwall is now more than 515,000 and there are 320,000 cars and vans registered in the county and available for use by households. 40,000 other vehicles are registered in the county, including everything from commercial vehicles to motorcycles. Vehicle registrations grew by a huge 43% between 1995 and 2005, and the average age of these vehicles is 7.8 years. In addition, more than 5 million visitors arrive in the county each year and August traffic flows are 60% higher than in January and 28% higher than the year-round daily average. However, it must be recorded that 20% of Cornish households do not own a car.

Once internal-combustion-engined motor cars appeared on the scene it was not long before commercial vehicles were conveying all manner of payloads throughout the county. For example, in 1910 the GWR introduced the first motor parcels van and in the 1920s 'Country Lorry Centres' were established with a GWR lorry fleet of some 100 vehicles. There were of course a growing number of private carriers. In this delightful scene from 1935/6 the Cornwall County Library Service has posed its brand new van, CV 8851 (a Cornish registration), beside Mount's Bay for this publicity shot. *Cornish Studies Library*

The total road mileage in Cornwall is 4,651 and, give or take a mile, that amount of space is finite, while vehicle usage is not. Although the holiday season is getting longer, therefore slightly flattening the peak periods, car ownership in Cornwall is growing. On a single summer's day 33,600 cars and 2,380 heavy commercial vehicles use the A30 Bodmin bypass. Between Liskeard and Dobwalls on the A38, 25,300 cars and 1,660 lorries pass by daily, with no fewer than 15,000 cars and 560 lorries travelling south of Wadebridge on the A39 and 14,300 cars and 450 lorries running between St Austell and Truro on the A390. Not surprisingly, Cornwall County Council has stated that, notwithstanding road improvements, many towns and traffic 'hot spots' will continue to suffer from traffic congestion. Clearly the image of sleepy Cornwall is changing fast!

The commercial vehicle scene reflects the virtual elimination of freight carried by rail in Cornwall, with the sole exception of china clay. The same situation applies to shipping where, in stark contrast to past decades and centuries, only a handful of bulk loads arrive by sea and, with the exception of china clay, coastal traffic is minimal. Except for a couple of trains per week handling special loads, every single commodity, from refrigerators to cornflakes, from armchairs to eggcups, is conveyed by road in heavy goods vehicles. Also, in terms of all road traffic generally, it should be pointed out that there is no viable alternative in many of Cornwall's remote villages and settlements. The car and the lorry are here to stay. The only decline in road transport has been the number of public service vehicles on the roads, which have reduced by 17% in just over

It did not take Cornish companies long to realise that for speed, efficiency and above all flexibility the potential of the commercial vehicle was immensely attractive. Many companies quickly developed their own lorry and van fleets and with improving roads they could collect and deliver merchandise just about anywhere in the county. This wonderful line-up from the 1930s represents the fleet of Stephens & Pope Ltd of St Austell. Behind is a reminder of the railway's presence. *Cornish Studies Library*

A/153188   TRENANCE CARAVAN & CHALET PARK, NEWQUAY

Over the years the popularity of caravanning has increased, although the impact on the average speed of holiday traffic remains controversial in some quarters. The vehicles provide an element of freedom for owners but also certain constraints. Whether towed by their owners or as static holiday accommodation, the appearance of caravans in parks or on cliff tops is not always aesthetically appealing. Cornwall has more than its share of caravans and this park at Trenance, Newquay, shows a typical installation, with the railway branch line on the extreme right. *Author's collection*

a decade, even though 30% of all bus routes in Cornwall are part funded by the County Council. The justification for using council taxpayers' and the heavily taxed motorists' money in this way is, thankfully, not for debate here, but perhaps the villages should continue to have a transport lifeline.

Finally, one interesting road transport scheme is enjoying its 40th birthday. In 1968 British Railways did a deal with the English China Clays company whereby BR closed its single-track branch line from Par Bridge at St Blazey to the docks at Fowey and in

Despite road improvements over the past century, many minor roads in Cornwall still run between the hedgerows and embankments with traffic relying on passing loops when encountering oncoming vehicles. In the heart of china clay country, between Carthew and St Dennis, these two 32-tonners gently pass each other with at least a foot between the rear view mirrors, on a road that is only just fit for purpose. *Author*

return ECC made certain guarantees about annual china clay tonnage rates that it would convey by rail. The railway line was lifted and converted into a road for the exclusive use of heavy ECC (now Imerys) lorries travelling from the central clay-drying plant at Par Harbour to the shipping point and store at Carne Point, Fowey. The scheme kept vast numbers of HGVs off the public roads and the lorries were not delayed by other traffic or vice versa, a 'win-win' situation.

Buses

It is strange to relate that the history of motorbuses in Cornwall is associated with a railway company. The Great Western Railway was a pioneer in the field of rural bus services in Cornwall, realising that, to provide connections to and from its main line and certain branch-line termini, the motorbus was the most cost-effective solution. With improved roads and the abolition of 19th-century road tolls, the cost of providing a bus service was insignificant when compared with the capital cost of providing a branch line. The bus was also more flexible than the train and could reach parts that other modes of public transport could not. Instead of passengers alighting at a station that was sometimes a mile or two from the nearest village, the bus provided an almost door-to-door service.

One of the first omnibus operators in Cornwall was the Great Western Railway, which really was a pioneer in the business, operating a service between Helston and the Lizard, the most southerly point on the UK mainland, as early as August 1903. By 1904 the company had expanded its services to many rural and formerly inaccessible parts of the county, operating 34 buses! In this wonderful animated shot, taken outside Penzance station in 1904 with, perhaps, the inaugural Marazion to Lands End service, bus crews and passengers pose for what would turn out to be an historic photograph. *M. Dart collection*

Postally used from Falmouth to Truro in June 1908, this evocative postcard depicts a scene outside Hill's Hotel at the Lizard a few years earlier. The GWR bus on the right carries the registration AF 66 and the one on the left is AF 84; both are chain-driven Milnes-Daimlers. The veteran car is AF 18, and in view are bus crews, passengers, small girls, a hotel waiter and the local 'bobby'. The Post Office can be glimpsed down the side street. *Author's collection*

The first GWR bus service commenced from Helston to the Lizard in August 1903, and by 1904 the company's Cornish fleet amounted to 34 vehicles, the first being made by Milnes-Daimler with 16hp and 20hp engines. The bus services were an immediate success, although the same cannot be said of the reliability of the vehicles themselves.

The brakes on the early buses were very inefficient and the wheel brake comprised a wooden shoe crudely rubbing on the solid rear tyres. There were three separate speed-change levers for the chain drive, and two glass oil bottles on the dashboard had to be kept topped up, even when on the move. On occasions horses would be employed to get the buses back to base. A few vehicles were modified to operate as 'luggage omnibuses'; passengers paid a lower fare on these semi-goods vehicles, which carried all manner of freight and even livestock! Slowly bus reliability improved and many of the original fleet were converted into goods lorries and parcels vans.

The GWR did not rest on its laurels and expanded its bus network to cover much of south-west Cornwall. At the end of 1904 the GWR had 34 buses and a year later this had more than doubled to 72. By 1905 the figure was 80, and in January 1908 the fleet numbered 113. As time went by buses increased in size and improved in reliability terms. By the 1920s the GWR had become one of the largest bus operators in the country, when a challenge to the legality of its operations was submitted by the road transport industry. It was claimed that the GWR did not have Parliamentary approval to operate road services. The GWR remedied the situation and in 1928 a Great Western Railway (Road Transport) Act was passed, which allowed the company to continue its operations but also to enter into agreements with other road transport operators. Consequently the GWR acquired a major interest in the National Omnibus & Transport Company, and from 1929 it transferred its entire bus fleet in the far South West to that company, which then operated under the newly created Western National Omnibus Company. From 1905 there was also a the Southern National Omnibus Company which had some links to the LSWR/Southern Railway.

There is not space to detail the GWR routes, but suffice to say that from 44 routes in 1920 the network grew to 154 routes in 1928. Subsequently the Western National company dominated the motorbus scene in Cornwall for decades, but there were other operators, such as Cornwall Motor Transport, which operated a large number of routes. With the advent of tourism, fostered by the railways from the late 1890s, came the local coach tour and day excursion, which was a very lucrative business in the summer months. There was room for a number of independent bus and coach tour operators, mainly running minor niche routes and operating with a handful of vehicles. Some of these were taken over by Western National, such as Trelawney Tours of Penzance and Hockings Tours of

A rare survivor from 1934 is this Western National guide and timetable, which proudly proclaims on the cover 'Associated with the Great Western Railway'. Negotiations between the National Omnibus & Transport Co and the Great Western Railway ended in agreement in December 1928 to merge the railway bus services and the National bus services into a railway related groups. From 1 January 1929 the GWR transferred all of its buses to Western National. *Author's collection*

Newquay. In 1928 through coach services from London to Bude, Penzance and Newquay commenced. In 1931 Western and Southern National were taken over by Thomas Tilling Ltd. There were significant takeovers and buyouts throughout the 1930s until the start of the Second World War. There was consolidation during the war years and bus mileage was cut by 40% due, in part, to fuel shortages.

After the Second World War business boomed until about 1953, the peak of Western/Southern National achievement. Petrol rationing ended, the number of cars increased, there was wage inflation and between 1951 and 1979 there were no fewer than 34 increases in bus fares! Services contracted and passenger numbers shrank by about 4% per annum. Many evening and Sunday services died out. One-man operation became widespread from 1957 as an economy measure and many outstations were closed. Western/Southern National engaged in severe cost-cutting in the 1970s and it was almost an irony that, following deregulation legislation in the late 1970s, independent operators started to appear in profusion. By 1986 there were no fewer than 34 bus and coach operators based in Cornwall! Mention must be made of the changes in technology as rear and underfloor engines, fully automatic gearboxes, power steering and low floors were all incorporated in contemporary bus design.

Some of these new operators have themselves taken over smaller operators and grown rapidly in a relatively short space of time to become sizeable companies operating large fleets of buses. For example, Western Greyhound and the recently taken over Truronian, both founded and run by former National Bus Company managers, have had remarkable growth records. Rural Challenge money became available in December 1998 and this encouraged smaller operators. Other companies have found niche markets in school and contract work, while others specialise in a compact geographical area of the county. The First Western National company and now FirstGroup continue to operate a number of major routes, but many minor local services still run, operated by privateers to sometimes eccentric timetables. The only major concern is that, with 30% of all Cornish bus routes receiving a subsidy from Cornwall County Council and with fuel costs escalating, any new pressure on public expenditure could see a further round of closures, whatever political directives emerge regarding free bus passes.

Over the years the Western and Southern National companies went on an amazing acquisition trail and between 1929 and 1978 took over more than 100 local bus and coach companies in the West Country. However, during the 1970s there was a period of severe cost-cutting by Western National, which resulted in a regeneration of independent operators. Here Western National No 3365, a single-deck Leyland Lion LT2, registration number VE 3783, refitted with a Beadle B34R body and Gardner engine, is destined for Falmouth Moor in about 1954. *Author's collection*

Many pre-Second World War buses soldiered on in service for several years after the war, including this Western National Bristol L5G, seen calling at Bodmin General station (SX 073664) in 1947, proving that integrated transport is not a recent phenomenon. The station building survived closure and is now the home of the thriving Bodmin & Wenford Railway, which runs steam and diesel services to Bodmin Parkway (Road) and Boscarne Junction. *Cornish Studies Library*

This vintage view shows both single- and double-deck Western National half-cabs, thought to be at Truro in the late 1930s. On the left is FJ 8958, fleet number 128, a 1931 Bristol H type with a B32R 32-seat Brush body, while on the right is DG 2671, fleet number 3128, a 1931 Leyland Titan TD1 with a Strachan H24/24R 48-seat body. Both buses were rebodied in 1942. *Courtesy of J. Hicks*

Above: Over the years there have been large numbers of minor bus and coach companies throughout Cornwall. Many were absorbed by the major companies, such as Southern and Western National, in both the 1930s and the early 1950s. However, after cost-cutting by the major operators in the 1970s and government legislation in the 1990s, the independents were encouraged and grew in number. One of the firms that survived the upheaval was Harveys of Mousehole. Seen here in 1972, the company's Bristol LH with a Marshall body had just arrived at Penzance. On many minor country routes short-wheelbase buses were the only practical solution to narrow roads and tight bends. *Bill Walker*

Below: Interesting transport stories do not always belong to the past. Formed at the end of 1997 by two ex-FirstGroup managers, Western Greyhound has become an important player in the Cornish bus transportation scene. Having taken over Cornishman Coaches, followed by R&M Coaches (which occupied the old Hawkeys Motors offices in Newquay) and later Pleasure Travel mini-coaches, the company took over the old Harris Coaches yard at Summercourt and has never looked back. A single-deck Mercedes midibus and a Volvo Olympian double-decker are seen at the bus station in their home town of Newquay in 2007. *Author*

Truronian was formed in 1987 by three former Western National managers. They took over Truronian Tours, Flora Motors, City Taxis of Truro and Williams of St Agnes. As with Western Greyhound, the company grew substantially running 68 buses with an annual turnover of £8.5

million before being taken over by FirstGroup in December 2008. From 1998 Rural Challenge cash became available and many small bus companies in Cornwall benefited. Here one of Truronian's Optare Solo buses is seen at Truro in March 2007 on the Portreath run. *Author*

With the town of St Ives in the background, local and national bus companies are represented. A Western Greyhound Volvo Olympian double-

decker in new livery stands beside a Transbus Dart of FirstGroup. Most of the passengers will comprise bus-pass-toting pensioners. *Author*

Railways

Early railways

The use of rails to transport ore and material in Cornish mines pre-dated the first attempts at building a tramway. Some of these mine tramways were quite lengthy, but it is generally accepted that the first tramway in Cornwall was the Poldice Tramway (also known as the Portreath Tramway), which was built from 1809 and part opened in 1812, as mentioned in the section on Portreath. The Poldice Tramway may have been the first built, but it was also one of the first to close due to a recession in the mining industry and competition from the West Cornwall Railway.

The second major undertaking connected Redruth and the mines in the Parish of Gwennap with the quayside at Devoran on Restronguet Creek. The line was proposed by mining entrepreneur John Taylor, who had little trouble in financing the £20,000 capital requirement. The only serious objection to his plan came from the Williams family, who had a major stake in the rival Poldice line. The relevant Act received Royal Assent on 17 June 1824 and the Redruth & Chasewater Railway was born. The line would run via Carharrack, Twelveheads, Bissoe and Carnon Mills, crossing the Truro to Falmouth road on the level.

Cornwall was at the forefront of mineral railways and tramways. The early lines were planned to address the chronic problem of transporting ores and minerals to the various ports for shipment and in making back runs with coal and timber for the pits and mines. An early line was the Redruth & Chasewater Railway; opened in 1824/5 with horse traction, it was upgraded in 1854 so that steam locomotives could be used. An 0-4-0ST (from 1856 0-4-2ST) called *Smelter*, built by Neilson & Co of Glasgow, was delivered to Devoran in November 1854, and during 1864 it covered 5,715 miles. The line closed in 1915 and the locomotive was scrapped in about 1918. *Ian Allan Library*

Another early line was the narrow-gauge Pentewan Railway, which ran from St Austell down to the harbour at Pentewan (see the earlier section on Pentewan). The line was opened in 1829 and was used primarily for the transportation of china clay outbound and coal inbound, although many other commodities were conveyed. In 1873/4 the line was converted from 4ft 6in to 2ft 6in gauge and steam locomotives replaced horses on most of the route. In this 1910 photograph at Iron Bridge, a Sunday excursion train is seen on the freight-only line, with passengers, and the band, being accommodated in china clay wagons. *Author's collection*

The 4-foot-gauge wrought-iron track was duly prepared and the line was officially opened on 30 January 1826. Tolls were determined on a ton/mile basis and all wagons were horse-drawn over most of the 9½ mile line, with a brakeman controlling any gravity working. There was a branch to Wheal Basset, part of a huge mining complex (see page 22). The railway was a great success and transportation costs were halved for the mine-owners. As early as 1830 the railway was hauling 60,000 tons per annum and making a £3,000 profit. It is estimated that about 20 small ships were using Devoran each week.

The standard-gauge horse-operated Treffry Tramways were opened in the 1840s but the famous entrepreneur did not live to see his objective of joining the north and south coasts of Cornwall by rail realised. This was finally achieved by the Cornwall Minerals Railway in 1874, and its steam locomotive fleet was housed in a special semi-roundhouse at St Blazey. Although no longer used by the railways, the striking listed red-brick building survives at SX 074537 and is now used by local light industries. The railway and turntable are located to the right of this view. *Author*

In 1838 competition arrived in the shape of the Hayle Railway branch from Hayle to Tresavean Mine. Between 1840 and 1850 tonnages were down and haulage rates were cut, resulting in a 20% fall in company profits.

By 1852 the railway had made £70,000 in 28 years. In 1853 the horses on the line moved a record 97,764 tons, but by the end of the year two steam locomotives had arrived to work the line. In 1857 the locomotives each covered 11,000 miles, but the output from many mines had peaked and in the following year a profit of only £658 was made. The last good year was 1864, when the locomotives covered 23,000 miles hauling 1,100 trains in each direction, about four per working day. The Poldice Tramway closed about 1865 and the last Gwennap mine closed in 1870, resulting in a steady decline. In 1877 the volume was just 36,000 tons and the total profit £72! Devoran kept silting up and costs were rising. Eventually there was no money left to pay for renewals. The company went into Receivership in 1884, but continued working. In 1907 the Basset mines were still using 15,000 tons of coal per annum, but by 1915 only 6,491 tons was hauled in a six-month period and the line closed forever on 25 September 1915.

The next line to open was the Pentewan Railway in 1829. The next important milestone was the opening of the standard-gauge Bodmin & Wadebridge Railway, which ran from Wadebridge to Ruthern Bridge, Bodmin (later Bodmin North) and Wenford Bridge (see pages 36 and 180). The B&WR was the first line in Cornwall to use steam locomotives. The Hayle Railway opened in 1837 (see pages 125 and 160), and the quaint Liskeard & Caradon Railway opened in stages between 1844 and 1846.

Another of Cornwall's fascinating early railways was the Liskeard & Caradon Railway, which originally ran from Moorswater to the various mines and quarries around Caradon Hill. It was extended to Looe and operated as the Liskeard & Looe Railway from 1860. This view at Looe was taken between 1886 and 1901 and shows Gilkes & Co 0-6-0ST *Kilmar* with two Liskeard & Caradon four-wheeled coaches and a brake-van. Note the lack of weather protection for the driver. *P. Q. Treloar* collection

This was another line that was worked by horses and gravity before locomotives appeared from 1862 (see page 37). One other undertaking worth mentioning in this chapter is the Cornwall Minerals Railway, which in 1873/4 took over, rebuilt and extended the 1841 to 1857 Treffry Tramways, opening a route from Fowey to Newquay together with mineral branches. The remarkable CMR works, roundhouse and turntable survive at St Blazey, as illustrated, and are well worth a visit. The CMR was worked by the GWR from 1877 and completely taken over by that company in 1896.

Broad gauge

As with his Great Western, Bristol & Exeter and South Devon Railways, Brunel also built the Cornwall Railway's main line, initially from Plymouth to Truro, to the broad gauge with longitudinal sleepers. The broad gauge was set to 7ft 0¼ in, which was of course not compatible with other railway companies, including the West Cornwall Railway, which was operating its standard gauge line from Penzance to Truro Road from 1852 and to Newham in 1855. The rails, at 62lb per yard, were on the light side for the traffic and frequent derailments were recorded, the first being just two days after the line opened in May 1859.

From 1859 the Cornish main line was run by two companies, the Cornwall Railway from Saltash to Truro and the West Cornwall Railway from Penzance to Truro and Newham. The former was built to the broad gauge (7ft 0¼ in) and the latter to 'narrow' (later standard) gauge (4ft 8½ in). It was not until 1867 that the first broad-gauge passenger train ran from one end of the county to the other. However, the broad gauge was doomed and full conversion to standard gauge took place in 1892. Here ex-South Devon Railway broad gauge 0-6-0ST No 2165 *Achilles* is seen at Penzance. It was rebuilt to standard gauge in 1893 and renumbered GWR No 1324. *P. Q. Treloar collection*

This is a truly historic photograph, showing the very last up GWR broad-gauge passenger train at Truro in May 1892. The double-headed working features 0-6-0ST No 1256 of 1877 vintage and 0-4-4BT No 3557 (formerly an 0-4-2ST). In their time both locomotives were converted from one gauge to another and both survived the imminent gauge change, after rebuilding. Note the enclosed overbridge and the water tank. *Brunel University*

In 1859 the Cornwall and the West Cornwall shared the same station at Truro, but due to the change of gauge any passengers travelling west of Truro had to change trains. The Falmouth branch opened in 1863, although it was then regarded as the Cornwall Railway's Plymouth to Falmouth 'main line'. It too was laid to broad gauge, as were a handful of later branches, the St Ives branch, which opened in 1877, being the last to be built to broad gauge specification. In 1864 the Cornwall Railway considered that the break in gauge at Truro was costing it money and it invoked a clause contained in the West Cornwall Act requiring the West Cornwall Railway to lay down a third rail all the way to Penzance. However, the West Cornwall were barely making ends meet and simply could not afford the permanent way work required, so the Associated Companies that owned the Cornwall Railway took over control from 1 January 1866. A huge amount of work was required, especially widening cuttings and embankments, but nevertheless broad-gauge goods trains started running in November 1866 and passenger trains in 1867, resulting in a mixed-gauge operation. By 1875 even the Cornwall Railway was struggling financially, and the GWR bailed out the company. Standard-gauge branches to Bodmin and Helston opened in 1887, and by that date there was less than full commitment to the broad gauge. Following the 1889 Bill of Amalgamation the GWR took over all operations. The Directors were well aware that the broad gauge had become a liability in that all goods and passengers had to be transhipped if they were travelling beyond the GWR main line. In any event, most of the GWR was by then mixed gauge, and thought had been given to the subject, designing locomotives and rolling stock as potentially 'convertible'.

All the necessary plans were therefore made and all broad-gauge stock was removed from the area by 19 May 1892. The entire line from Exeter to Truro, which had remained broad gauge only, was converted to 'narrow', or standard, gauge in two days, on Saturday 20 and Sunday 21 May. For the conversion nearly 5,000 men converged on Devon and Cornwall from all over the GWR network and were divided into gangs, each responsible for about 3½ miles of track. As an amusing aside, the Wills's tobacco company provided 5,000 2oz packets of 'Westward Ho' tobacco for the labourers. The work was completed on time, which must rank as one of the largest and certainly the most impressive permanent way projects ever undertaken in the UK, and an exercise that Network Rail could learn from! The anachronism of the broad gauge became history overnight.

Royal Albert Bridge

The Royal Albert Bridge has not only provided the primary rail link between Devon and Cornwall for 150 years but has also become a national icon as the grand entrance to the Royal Duchy. In aesthetic terms its imposing position across the mighty River Tamar was diluted in 1961 by the building of a concrete road bridge beside it, which was larger than the veteran railway bridge. But in terms of style it was no contest, Isambard Kingdom Brunel's design winning by a country mile!

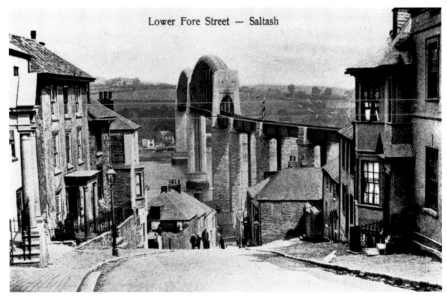

Perhaps the most significant railway icon in the whole of Cornwall is the 1859-built Royal Albert Bridge that spans the mighty River Tamar. The bridge is inextricably linked with the famous engineer Isambard Kingdom Brunel, whose name is emblazoned on the structure. Originally designed for double track, £100,000 was saved by the cash-strapped Cornwall Railway by opting for a single-track structure. In this early view the magnificent bridge is seen from Lower Fore Street, Saltash. *Author's collection*

Although Brunel witnessed the first truss of the bridge being floated into position, he was not well enough to attend the formal opening on 2 May 1859 and sadly died later in the year. It has been claimed that this structure was his finest railway bridge and it has recently celebrated its 150th anniversary. It is many years since lower-quadrant semaphore signals were in place on the Royal Albert Bridge, but back in Edwardian times, with a wonderful rake of clerestory coaches in tow, a GWR 4-4-0 leaves the structure at Saltash with a down train. *Author's collection*

The original legislation stipulated that the Cornwall Railway should cross the Tamar by a high-level bridge rather than a steam ferry. Brunel selected a location where the river narrowed, making the building of the bridge easier and cheaper. Unfortunately the Admiralty, which has always had a strong presence in nearby Devonport, insisted that any bridge needed to be 100 feet above the waterline to allow tall ships to pass beneath. Various design configurations were considered before the final option was selected, comprising two main spans of 455 feet each with a single central pier, seven additional arches on the Devon side, and ten arches on the Cornish side, all 17 being on a curved alignment. This was to be the largest engineering project of its time.

The central pier was all-important and took much of the stress. However, there was 70 feet of water and 20 feet of mud laying between the surface of the water and the bedrock of the river. Brunel had had experience of working with a diving bell and compressed air when tunnelling under the River Thames, so such a device was used in constructing the foundations of the central pier. Brunel saved the Cornwall Railway £100,000 by designing the bridge for single track only. In 1853 a contract worth £162,000 was awarded to Messrs C. J. Mare, but the firm soon went bankrupt and Brunel decided to project-manage the construction of the bridge himself. In the meantime the Prince Consort, HRH Prince Albert, had agreed to have the bridge named after him.

There were problems in locating the bedrock, then building up from it, but these difficulties were overcome. The two main trusses were built on the Devon side of the river.

The wrought-iron work in each span weighed 1,600 tons. On 1 September 1857 the first of these great trusses was floated out to the base of the piers on pontoons. The entire operation was quite remarkable, but was based on a process first adopted with the Britannia Bridge over the Menai Strait. The day was a general holiday and an estimated 40,000 people watched the proceedings. The massive truss was lifted very slowly by hydraulic jacks, gaining 6 feet in height every week until it reached its final position in July 1858. The second truss was floated out and the entire proceedings went without a hitch; it reached its final position in March 1859. The approach spans were ordinary girders supported on granite piers and they were being built while the main trusses were being worked on.

A test train crossed the bridge on 11 April 1859 and the remarkable structure was formally opened on 2 May 1859. The final statistics make interesting reading. The bridge was 2,200 feet long, it contained 2,650 tons of wrought iron, 1,200 tons of cast iron, 459,000 cubic feet of masonry and 14,000 cubic feet of timber.

The bridge was floodlit for its centenary in 1959 and more than a decade later it was strengthened. During 2006 some unsightly stairway scaffolding was removed to reveal the full lettering 'I. K. BRUNEL ENGINEER 1859'. The bridge recently celebrated its 150th anniversary.

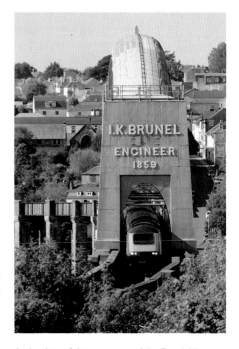

At the time of the centenary of the Royal Albert Bridge in 1959 the entire structure was floodlit and, with the 150th anniversary looming, Network Rail decided to remove some external walkway scaffolding that for years had obliterated the name of I. K. Brunel. Photographed with a 300mm Nikkor lens at just after 13.00, in order for the lighting to place the vast letters in relief, a First Great Western IC 125 crosses from Cornwall to Devon with a Penzance to Paddington train in September 2007. *Author*

The Age of Steam

In the early days of the West Cornwall Railway (WCR) and Cornwall Railway (CR) main lines there was a remarkable miscellany of standard-gauge and broad-gauge locomotives working in Cornwall. Prior to the 1859 opening the estimated motive power requirement for broad-gauge engines was eight passenger and two goods locomotives (later reduced to one) to work all trains between Plymouth and Truro. The locomotives were to be provided by Evans & Company, the contractor for the neighbouring South Devon Railway (SDR). A very precise performance specification was produced and brand-new locomotives were to be provided, 4-4-0 bogie saddle tanks

Above: For many readers their first vivid recollections of steam trains on BR will date back to the late 1950s. For a lucky few it will be holidays in Cornwall that will be recalled. One of the great charms of the Cornish railway scene was the profusion of branch lines and junction stations where passengers would change to reach their chosen holiday destination. In this thoroughly charming scene, recorded at Lostwithiel on 22 September 1959, the crew of the little Fowey branch train have time for a chat before the next branch working. The locomotive is one of the quaint-looking Collett 0-4-2Ts, No 1419 of St Blazey depot, working just two coaches. The line closed to passengers just six years later. *P. Q. Treloar*

Above: For many the days of steam in Cornwall were memorable, substantially based on an association with the classic and glamorous GWR 4-6-0 classes working named trains. The most famous of all Cornish trains was the 'Cornish Riviera', and what a remarkable train it was. With a massive 14 coaches in tow, 'Hall' class No 6940 *Didlington Hall* will have its work cut out on Cornwall's demanding main line. The train has just left Penzance on 17 April 1954. *B. K. B. Green*

Another well-known Cornish named train was 'The Cornishman', which worked between Penzance and Yorkshire. One of the powerful 'County' class 4-6-0s, No 1010 *County of Caernarvon*, slogs up the 1 in 84/62 climb towards Treverrin Tunnel between Par and Lostwithiel on 31 July 1956. Note the '675' train reporting number, the two white oil lamps providing an 'express passenger' headcode and the cast metal nameboard on the upper smokebox door. *Les Elsey*

for passenger trains similar to those on the SDR, based on a Gooch/GWR design, and an 0-6-0ST for goods trains. Locomotive workshops were erected at Lostwithiel.

The Hayle Railway, the predecessor of the West Cornwall Railway, also engaged a contractor to provide motive power for its trains, which commenced operation in 1837. A total of six locomotives were provided, although details are sparse. One of the engines, *Cornubia*, was the first built in Cornwall at the Copperhouse Foundry. After being taken over by the WCR, more engines were required for the additional Redruth to Penzance services. Until 1865 there were up to 15 locomotives in service, comprising three tank and 12 tender engines, from three manufacturers. From 1866 until 1876 the actual operating side of the former WCR was the responsibility of the South Devon Railway and this brought a range of saddle tank locomotives into Cornwall. At the time of the handover to the GWR in 1876 there were six locomotives allocated to Penzance and three to Truro. Various engines of both broad and narrow gauge were used in Cornwall until the abolition of the broad gauge.

Classes of locomotives used from 1892 included '3521' 0-4-4Ts (later reconstructed as 4-4-0 tender engines), Armstrong 0-6-0s, 'Stella' 2-4-0s, 'Dean Goods' 0-6-0s, 'Duke' 4-4-0s, 'Bulldog' 4-4-0s, Churchward '43xx' and '63xx' 2-6-0s, '3150' 2-6-2Ts and '28xx' 2-8-0s, 'Aberdare' 2-6-0s, '61xx' 2-6-2Ts, and '42xx' and '72xx' heavy freight

2-8-0Ts and 2-8-2Ts. On the branch lines in the early days were a miscellany of 0-6-0STs and other classes, including the '1076' 0-6-0PTs, 'Metro' 2-4-0Ts, Armstrong '517' 0-4-2Ts, '2021' and '2181' 0-6-0PTs, '1366' 0-6-0STs, '44xx' 2-6-2Ts, the superb '45xx' 2-6-2Ts, '51xx' 2-6-2Ts, Churchward '57xx' 0-6-0PTs, and Hawksworth '16xx' and '94xx' 0-6-0PTs. Many other GWR classes appeared over the decades in addition to these stalwarts, and a variety of steam locomotives worked on industrial and dock lines.

London & South Western Railway classes must not be forgotten, and locomotives working in Cornwall over that company's lines, to Bude, Bodmin, Wadebridge and Padstow, included the following classes: '0298' 2-4-0WTs, 'X6' 4-4-0s, 'O2' 0-4-4Ts, 'M7' 0-4-4Ts, '0415' 4-2-2Ts, '0395' 0-6-0s, '0460' 4-4-0s, 'T9' 4-4-0s, 'L11' 4-4-0s, 'N' 2-6-0s, and 'WC' and 'BB' 4-6-2s. British Railways Standard classes and LMS types also appeared, including 3MT 2-6-2Ts, 4MT 2-6-4Ts and Ivatt 2-6-2Ts. In the early days PD&SWJR '757' class 0-6-2Ts and 0-6-0Ts worked on the Callington branch, and from time to time other Southern classes made appearances in Cornwall.

Of all the classes linked to steam in Cornwall, special mention must be made of the classic classes of GWR/BR(WR) 4-6-0s. With their gleaming brass nameplates and copper-banded chimneys, the 'Courts', 'Saints', 'Stars', 'Castles', 'Counties', 'Halls', 'Granges' and 'Manors' all worked in the Royal Duchy for many decades and on all types of train. The most memorable were the famous named trains such as the 'Cornish Riviera', the 'Royal Duchy' and the 'Cornishman'. One other class that must not be forgotten is the BR 'Britannia' 4-6-2s, which worked certain prestigious trains through to Penzance in the early 1950s.

The most graceful and handsome of the GWR 4-6-0s were the 'Castle' class locomotives. With its brass chimney band and safety valve cover glowing, a very clean No 7006 *Lydford Castle* of Plymouth's Laira depot passes Saltash with the up 'Cornish Riviera' Limited in July 1959. The station overbridge and both up and down awnings have long gone and the old chapel burned to the ground some years ago. *M. Dart collection*

One of the real workhorses of the steam age in Cornwall was the small-wheeled 'Grange' class of 4-6-0s. The class successfully worked every type of passenger and freight train in the Duchy for many years, but unlike other popular GWR classes not a single 'Grange' was preserved. In this typical 1950s scene No 6809 *Burghclere Grange* starts the down ex-Plymouth workman's train away from Liskeard on a fine June evening. *Michael Mensing*

There were many motive power depots and stabling points in Cornwall and most of the branch lines had small sub-sheds at their termini. However, the main depots were located at Wadebridge (72F), St Blazey (83E), Truro (83F) and Long Rock, near Penzance (83G). All had turntables, coaling and watering facilities. Some of the allocations were quite sizeable; for example, St Blazey had an allocation of 36 engines at times. In 1953 official outstations or sub-sheds were located at Launceston, Callington, Bodmin, Moorswater, Helston and St Ives. However, in earlier years locations such as Bude, Newquay and Falmouth (and many others) had small depots.

Since the end of steam in Cornwall during 1962 the world of preservation has been active, and whether on the Bodmin & Wenford Railway or at the head of main-line special trains, appearances of steam locomotives on standard-gauge Cornish tracks have since been regular occurrences. Visiting locomotives have been many and varied but perhaps one of the most notable achievements was in October 2006 when 'King' class 4-6-0 No 6024 *King Edward I* worked over the Royal Albert Bridge with the 'Cornubian' railtour. In the days of steam, route availability and weight restrictions prevented the class from entering Cornwall. In the early days there was an enormous variety of steam locomotives working on minor and mostly narrow-gauge lines and this scene is perpetuated today on the Lappa Valley Railway and the Launceston Steam Railway.

Branch lines

There is something romantic about country branch lines and in its heyday Cornwall had more than its share. Most of them were extremely scenic. Although some branches closed decades ago, the majority closed during the 1960s when the infamous Dr Beeching was implementing a rationalisation plan following a review of loss-making railway lines. Some of the lines that closed were hopelessly unremunerative with just a handful of passengers on each train. To that extent Beeching and his team, in other words the Government, were right to closely examine profitability.

However, what was significant by its absence was a detailed explanation of the cost basis used in their calculations, for example the value of notional permanent way replacement and depreciation on capital items. Also ignored was the scope for rationalisation within the existing operation, for example by singling the track, removing signalling or cutting staff. Arguably the greatest oversight was the absence of any debate about developing and maximising the potential of a branch. Today there are incentives to travel on the remaining branches such as line 'branding', brochures about their scenic attractions and things to see and do along the line, 'park and ride' schemes and even 'ale trails' and rover tickets. Unfortunately there are also examples of positive deterrents to travel, such as infrequent branch trains and a lack of important main-line connections.

Although less glamorous than their larger cousins, the various small Prairie 2-6-2Ts were attractive and purposeful steam locomotives that were particularly at home on Cornish branch lines. Heading away from Truro and destined for the Falmouth branch on 18 September 1957,

No 4554 has five wagons and a brake-van in tow as it climbs past the motive power depot towards Highertown Tunnel. Note the semaphore signals and the locomotive turntable to the left.
P. Q. Treloar

It is amazing to relate that half a century after the previous photograph was taken a preserved Western Region 2-6-2T Prairie steam locomotive was still at work in Cornwall. With the magnificent Glynn Valley as a backdrop, the Bodmin & Wenford Railway's beautifully restored No 5552 hauls a rake of maroon coaches (the Mark 2a examples short-sightedly since disposed of) past Charlie's Gate on its way from Bodmin Parkway to Bodmin General. The railway has a wonderful stable of both steam and diesel locomotives and is well worth a visit. *Author*

Although many lines were lost (see the next section), there were special issues to be considered in some cases and these factors saved some of Cornwall's most attractive branch lines. For example, the lack of road accessibility from Plymouth to Calstock and Gunnislake undoubtedly saved the branch, even though the Gunnislake to Callington section was closed. This scenic route crosses a number of attractive estuaries on the Devon side of the Tamar, with trains reversing at Bere Alston before entering the county of Cornwall by crossing the River Tamar on the spectacular Calstock Viaduct. The views of the Tamar and the profusion of old mining chimneys make for a fascinating ride.

Another factor taken into consideration was the enormous influx of visitors to Cornwall during the summer months. This almost certainly saved the Liskeard to Looe line. Branch trains leave Liskeard from their own station, set at right angles to the main-line station, and descend steeply to Coombe Junction, where they reverse before heading off to Looe. The ride down to the coast along the valley of the East Looe River is simply a delight. At places the valley is shared with a road, the river and an old abandoned canal.

The Newquay branch line is more than 20 miles long and traverses a remarkable variety of landscapes, ranging from the steep and heavily wooded Luxulyan Valley to the strange china clay tip industrial background around Bugle, and the rolling farmland on the final approaches to Cornwall's largest holiday resort on the north coast. Newquay is now the surfing capital of England and is served by the only Cornish branch line that still receives main-line through trains in the summer months from all over the UK, including Scotland.

The first main-line diesel locomotives arrived in Cornwall in 1958 and they were quickly followed by a number of diesel units for use on branch lines and local stopping services. A unique experiment in Cornwall during the early 1960s was the use of a four-wheeled railbus from Bodmin North to Boscarne Junction and also to Wadebridge. An AC railcars example is seen at the interchange platform at Boscarne Junction with an ex-Bodmin North working. *Blencowe collection*

The Falmouth branch was another survivor because over the entire year the traffic figures were higher than on other branches and there was a healthy commuter service, which removed at least some of the congestion on the A39 road. The branch connects two major centres of population and the ride is interesting, with two tunnels and several viaducts on the line and a superb view over Penryn on a clear day. At the end of the line is Falmouth Docks, which unfortunately does not produce any railfreight traffic.

The last survivor from the 1960s cull was the St Ives branch, which has always been heavily used in the summer months. Closure would have resulted in traffic chaos in the area for five months of the year. So busy were the roads that a 'park and ride' system was introduced whereby motorists left their cars at Lelant Saltings, where a new concrete station was opened, and rode the train to Carbis Bay and St Ives. The views along the Hayle estuary and the north coast are spectacular, as are the beaches along the way. The branch line survivors in Cornwall are all well worth a visit. Surviving freight only branches include Lostwithiel to Fowey and Burngullow to Parkandillack.

Closed lines

The number of lines that have been closed in Cornwall since the 1960s has been staggering. In addition to the swingeing so-called Beeching cuts of passenger branch lines there have been significant changes in industrial technology, the closure of freight installations and even a rail to road conversion, all resulting in line closures. In addition to complete line closures there have been scores of sidings and goods yards closed as well as a number of main-line stations. The closure list makes rather depressing reading.

Although Cornwall suffered from a number of line closures in the Beeching era of the 1960s, a number of branch lines survived, including the picturesque route from Liskeard to Looe, featured here. In the final years of the first-generation diesel-mechanical units, one example, Class 117 No 305, was painted in GWR chocolate and cream livery. It is seen on the banks of the East Looe River at Terras Pill (SX 248556) forming the 16.50 service from Looe on a September day in 1993 (see also page 85). *Author*

An experiment that went badly wrong occurred in 1986/7 when some new four-wheeled diesel units were imported for use on Cornish branch lines. The Class 142s had a long wheelbase, which was not compatible with the tight curves encountered, causing flange wear and squealing; moreover there was no sanding gear to assist with adhesion on wet greasy rails on gradients, and the doors were unreliable. Just before being transferred away in June 1987 No 142025 is seen at St Columb Road on the 20¾ mile Newquay branch with a down working. *Author*

Cornish lines closed since 1960 include: the Bude branch; the North Cornwall line from Okehampton in Devon to Wadebridge and Padstow; Wadebridge to Bodmin North, Bodmin General and Wenford Bridge; Bodmin Road to Bodmin General; the Launceston branch; Gunnislake to Callington; Lostwithiel to Fowey (open for freight); Fowey to St Blazey; the Ponts Mill line; the Goonbarrow branch; the Wheal Rose branch; the Carbis Wharf branch; the St Dennis Junction to Parkandillack line; the Retew branch; the Trenance Valley or Bojea branch; the Nanpean Wharf and Drinnick Mill (lower) branch; Penwithers Junction to Newham; Chacewater to Newquay; the Helston branch; the remains of the Roskear branch; and the Hayle Wharf branch. The Bodmin & Wenford Railway has saved and preserved two formerly closed lines from Bodmin General.

There are no other Cornish branch lines presently under threat. Two factors that have emerged in recent years that could help preserve the surviving lines are political pressure to maintain a public transport infrastructure and the recent obsession with global warming issues. However, when any observer looks at the handful of passengers on

The sun does not always shine in Cornwall; in fact, it can be very wet as weather fronts roll in off the Atlantic Ocean. With only the train conductor inappropriately dressed for the climatic conditions, heavy rain bounces off the platform at Penryn station in September 2005. Satisfying a useful local transport need is single-car Class 153 No 153382 with a Falmouth to Truro working. The station once had two platforms and a passing loop, substantial buildings and a goods yard, but all have been consigned to history. However in 2009 new arrangements were being made allowing branch trains to pass, thereby increasing line capacity. *Author*

This section of line from Coombe Junction to Moorswater closed to passengers in 1901 but remained open for freight into the 21st century. Formerly the site of a clay-drying plant and later a cement distribution depot, the line is still in situ. In this almost unbelievable image, 125-tonne Heavy Haul Freightliner No 66613 negotiates the weeds and is about to cross a minor country road with an inbound cement train in the autumn of 2004 (SX 236642). *Author*

Newquay branch workings during the winter months, it would be debatable whether a single taxi would emit more carbon than a Class 153 or 155 unit.

It never ceases to fascinate how quickly nature reclaims the land once a railway line closes. For example, already it is almost impossible to trace the Carbis Wharf branch line, which closed as recently as 1989. Some of the ancient closed railways on moorland that is grazed by sheep can still be traced almost a century after closure, thanks to their granite setts or sleepers. However, as illustrated, other lines are taken over by tree and plant growth and within three or four decades it is impossible to believe that a train ever

Some Cornish branch lines that were closed to passenger traffic in the 1960s survived as freight-only lines. A classic example is the line from Lostwithiel to Fowey, which runs along the banks of the River Fowey. Closed to passengers in 1965, the line has remained open for more than 40 years for use by china clay trains working to Carne Point, at Fowey Docks. A popular photographic vantage point is at the village of Golant, and powering past the harbour at low tide in October 2007 is No 66019 with a rake of empty CDA wagons in tow (SX 123548). *Author*

The closed railway lines and sidings all over Cornwall could fill a book in their own right. Featured here is the 1905-built Chacewater to Newquay line, a branch that has seen partial reuse. In this evocative view, taken in 2003, exactly 40 years after closure, the diminutive Mitchell & Newlyn Halt is featured (SX 833553). Remarkably, the concrete platform and its only structure, a crude corrugated-iron shelter, has survived the passage of time despite the encroaching foliage. *Author*

passed the location. On the other hand some track alignments have been converted to footpaths, such as the Camel Trail from Padstow to Bodmin and Wenford Bridge, and others have been converted to roads, such as Par Harbour to Fowey.

By far the best reuse for old railway lines is to build new railway lines on the abandoned trackbeds, and this is exactly what has happened in the case of part of the old Chacewater to Newquay branch line. Opened in 1974, the 15-inch-gauge Lappa Valley Railway, near Newlyn East, was built near the site of the old East Wheal Rose lead mine and is thus on the alignment of the original Treffry Tramway of 1849. This tourist line takes holidaymakers to further tourist attractions adjacent to the old engine house (see below).

In 1968 an enthusiast called Eric Booth had a vision to create a narrow-gauge tourist line on part of the old Chacewater to Newquay branch line. By June 1974 this vision had become a working 15-inch-gauge railway on an alignment that was part of the old 1849 Newquay Tramway from East Wheal Rose to Newquay Harbour, which considerably pre-dated the 1905 GWR branch line. In September 2003 No 1 *Zebedee* leaves Benny Halt (SX 837573) for East Wheal Rose, once the largest lead mine in Cornwall. *Author*

Viaducts

Cornwall is unique in so many aspects of industry and transport, and on no other main line anywhere in the UK are there so many viaducts per mile. Between Saltash and Penzance, a distance of just over 75 miles, there are a remarkable 40 viaducts with a total length of nearly 5 miles. Originally there were a further eight viaducts on the 1½-mile Falmouth branch. The topography of the Cornish countryside was such that one of the original plans to build a main line from Plymouth to Penzance included unacceptably sharp curves and gradients, and one even included an inclined plane, similar to those on the 1837 Hayle Railway from Hayle to Redruth. One of the reasons behind these rather extreme cost-saving plans was the difficulty in raising capital in the wake of earlier exuberance by investors in railways, known as "railwaymania".

Isambard Kingdom Brunel (1806-59) was charged in his capacity of Engineer of the Cornwall Railway with designing and building a main line from Plymouth to Falmouth via Truro. To be able to cross numerous estuaries, tidal creeks and river valleys it would be necessary to construct viaducts, many of them on curved alignments. He was already experienced in the use of timber for such structures, which in this case had to be cheap, cost-effective and fit for purpose. To achieve this objective he used much ingenuity in design, using both masonry and wood to the limits of mid-19th-century technology.

Between Saltash and Penzance there were originally 40 viaducts of note and a further eight on the Falmouth branch. To bridge the many river valleys the Cornwall Railway took a short-sighted but financially necessary course of building cheap but effective viaducts, using largely timber structures mostly on masonry piers. Many of these structures were designed by Brunel and his successor Brereton. They were up to 150 feet high and several were on curved alignments. Ponsanooth on the Falmouth branch was a 645-foot-long, 139-foot-high Margary Class B structure with eight large fully buttressed piers. It was replaced in 1931. A Falmouth branch train, with five six-wheelers and a bogie coach visible, crosses the structure in about 1904. *P. Q. Treloar collection*

Although in retrospect certain aspects of the design could be criticised, some viaducts having to be replaced after only 16 years, there is no doubt that, with others lasting nearly 75 years and with the piers of some viaducts still in daily use, there cannot have been that much wrong with the fundamentals. Certainly there were complaints from passengers as trains swayed on the graceful but perhaps marginally flexible structures, and it is said that they creaked and groaned as trains crossed, but without Brunel's input there would have been no Cornwall Railway main line. Whether the adulation afforded to him in respect of his timber works is justified, only an engineer could say, because in North America there were 19th-century wooden structures that made some of Brunel's creations look quite puny – but perhaps that is the point.

In order from Saltash to Penzance and from Truro to Falmouth, the original viaducts (with their length and height in feet) were as follows:

Coombe by Saltash	(603/86)	Fal	(570/90)
Forder	(606/67)	Probus	(435/43)
Wiveliscombe	(198/25)	Tregarne	(606/83)
Grove	(114/29)	Tregagle	(315/69)
Nottar	(921/67)	Truro	(1,329/92)
St Germans	(945/106)	Carvedras	(969/86)
Tresulgan	(525/93)	Penwithers	(372/54)
Coldrennick	(795/138)	Chacewater	(297/52)
Treviddo	(486/101)	Blackwater	(396/68)
Cartuther	(411/98)	Redruth	(489/61)
Bolitho	(546/113)	Penponds	(693/45)
Liskeard	(720/150)	Angarrack	(798/100)
Moorswater	(954/147)	Guildford	(384/56)
Westwood	(372/88)	Hayle	(831/34)
St Pinnock	(633/151)	Penzance	(1,041/12)
Largin	(567/130)		
West Largin	(315/75)	Penwithers	(813/90)
Draw Wood	(669/42)	Ringwell	(366/70)
Derrycombe	(369/77)	Carnon	(756/96)
Clinnick	(330/74)	Perran	(339/56)
Penadlake	(426/42)	Ponsanooth	(645/139)
Milltown	(501/75)	Pascoe	(390/70)
St Austell	(720/115)	Penryn	(342/83)
Gover	(690/95)	Collegewood	(954/100)
Coombe St Stephens	(738/70)		

It should be noted that Wiveliscombe, Grove, Nottar and St Germans (original) were all on an old alignment abandoned in 1908. Penzance Viaduct was demolished and a new embankment built on reclaimed land in 1921. On the Falmouth branch, Penwithers, Ringwell, Pascoe and Penryn were all replaced by embankments.

Cornwall's fine viaducts dominate the landscape in several areas, some are hidden away from main roads and access points, while others are shrouded in trees and foliage.

Forder Viaduct below Trematon Castle is accessible from a minor road that runs down the nearby tidal creek. The view of St Germans Viaduct from St Germans quay is impressive and, while visiting, it is worth exploring the nearby lime kilns. Coldrennick Viaduct can be seen from the main A38 road, but the best view is alongside a 'no stopping' area. The high Liskeard Viaduct is best seen from the Looe branch line or an

Above: In this spectacular view of Collegewood Viaduct, south of Penryn on the Falmouth branch, recorded on 30 January 1934, the original Brereton curved timber-topped structure is being replaced by a new masonry viaduct. This was the last of the original viaducts to survive, but had apparently been in rather a poor state of repair for some time. The viaduct was 100 feet above the floor of the valley (SX 781343). The crane on the right is running on its own steeply graded narrow-gauge track. *GWR/Ian Allan Library*

Right: One of the joys of photographing trains in the Cornish landscape is incorporating the remains of the original viaducts in the picture. A good example can be found at Coombe St Stephens Viaduct, about 5 miles west of St Austell (SW 944512). Crossing the structure on 17 April 1985 is No 50006 *Neptune* with empty cement tankers from Chacewater. The old ivy-covered piers can be seen below the train. *Author*

industrial estate in Liskeard. There is a fine view of Moorswater Viaduct from many side roads in the area and the remains of the old original Brunel masonry piers are well worth seeking out, if only to marvel at their size. The Glynn Valley between Doublebois and Bodmin Parkway is heavily wooded and most of the viaducts have been obscured. However, from the Trago Mills car park and from a nearby footpath the view of the incredible masonry piers of St Pinnock Viaduct, which are original and still in use today, 150 years after being built, is tremendous.

St Austell Viaduct dominates the western side of the town and is easy to locate and view, but further west the impressive Coombe St Stephen Viaduct requires a traipse across farmland for the best view, but only with permission. The two huge viaducts in Truro completely dominate the northern part of the city. Angarrack Viaduct can be gazed at from below, in the village of the same name; indeed, there is a fine public house below the viaduct and nearby an old road sign reads 'Gwinear Road Sta. ¾'. Hayle Viaduct looks quaint as it stands above the road to St Erth on the western side of the town. The most impressive viaduct on the Falmouth branch is Collegewood, easily found and seen just south of Penryn station.

There were also a number of viaducts on many of Cornwall's branches, the most impressive being Calstock Viaduct on the Gunnislake branch, Ponts Mill and the Treffry Viaduct in the Luxulyan Valley, Trenance Viaduct on the Newquay branch, and Carbis Bay Viaduct on the St Ives branch. Other viaducts could be found on many of the closed lines (see the previous section).

This delightful view shows one of Cornwall's most graceful viaducts, St Germans, just east of the village and station of the same name. Crossing the River Tiddy 100 feet above the tiny harbour is a Virgin Trains 'Voyager' unit forming the 09.30 Penzance to Glasgow service on 12 September 2007. This viaduct was ready for service in 1908 when a new main-line alignment opened and an older wooden viaduct to the south was demolished. This view is possible from the A374 road to Torpoint at SW 363566, with the aid of a medium telephoto lens. *Author*

Moorswater Viaduct near Liskeard is, without doubt, one of the most spectacular in Cornwall by virtue of its height and the open views that can be obtained from the A38 road. Also, the remains of several of the Gothic-arched apertures of the original pre-1881 viaduct are clearly visible (centre and centre right). Crossing this wonderful curved structure is Freightliner's No 66613 with empty Cargowaggons and tankers in September 2004, heading west in order to 'run round' before returning to Earle's Sidings in Derbyshire. *Author*

Modern traction

The word 'modern' seems hardly appropriate, because it is now half a century since main-line diesel locomotives arrived in the Royal Duchy. In the British Railways 1955 Modernisation Plan the South West was selected for complete dieselisation at an early date. The Western Region (WR) had a preference for diesel locomotives with hydraulic transmission, whereas the BR standard was to become diesel-electric. The German railways had considerable experience and technical expertise in the field of diesel-hydraulics and to the WR Board it seemed logical to look in that direction. Consequently the diesel engines and the transmissions for its new generation of locomotives were German but made under licence in the UK. Elsewhere on BR early classes and prototypes mostly had the diesel-electric specification.

The first diesel locomotives ordered for the WR all came from the North British Locomotive Company (NBL) and included five large A1A-A1A twin-engined 2,000hp locomotives and six B-B single-engined 1,000hp machines. The large 117-ton locomotives were all named after warships of the Royal Navy; the first, No D600 *Active*, hauled its maiden revenue-earning train in February 1958 (they were later designated Class 41). In July 1958 the first of the far more nimble 78-ton 2,000hp B-B main-line diesel locomotives, also known as and named after warships, was delivered. The Swindon-built locomotives had Maybach engines and Mekydro transmissions, and those examples built by NBL at Glasgow were fitted with German MAN engines and Voith transmissions. Mostly rated at 2,200hp, they would become Class 42 and 43.

Also arriving in 1958 was the first of the 65-ton 1,000hp locomotives, later upgraded to 1,100hp and weighing 68 tons, which became known as Class 22.

By January 1959 the last of the original five large 'Warships' had been delivered and the smaller 'Warships' and NBL Type 2s were arriving in Cornwall, although mostly allocated to Laira depot at Plymouth. The small Type 2s often worked main-line expresses in double-headed mode, but they were also employed on branch freight and passenger trains, particularly to Callington and on both lines to Newquay. The two types of 'Warship' handled main-line trains, but by the 1960s the first of the large 136-ton 1Co-Co1 'Peak' Class 45 diesel-electrics began to appear on inter-regional workings. They were fitted with 2,500hp Sulzer engines and Crompton Parkinson traction motors and electrical equipment.

In 1962 the first of the 'Rolls-Royce' of diesel-hydraulic locomotives, the 108-ton twin-engined 2,700hp Type 4 'Westerns', entered Cornwall. These locomotives dominated the Paddington to Penzance main line and 74 examples were delivered between the very end of 1961 and mid-1964. They were later to become Class 52. In the meantime diesel-mechanical multiple-units had replaced steam on all branch-line workings. Diesel shunters were also imported, replacing elderly steam locomotives. In 1964/65 1,700hp B-B 'Hymek' diesel-hydraulics made incursions into Cornwall but they could never be regarded as natives.

In 1967 the ubiquitous 117-ton Co-Co Sulzer-engined 2,750hp (later regulated to 2,580hp) Brush Type 4s, or Class 47s, arrived in Cornwall, and this was the start of an association with the county that lasted for more than 40 years. Although seen mainly on Class 1 passenger trains, they also performed a mixed-traffic role and could

This view is the epitome of the modern china clay scene in Cornwall. English, Welsh & Scottish Railway (now DB Schenker) owned, North American-built, 3,200hp computer-controlled Class 66 No 66241 arrives at Par with a train of air-braked 'Tiger' and tanker wagons. Not so modern are the splendid lower-quadrant semaphore signals that control rail movements in this area. These superb locomotives haul what would, until 1999, have been regarded as double-length trains with a gross weight of 1,900 tonnes. *Author*

The first main-line diesels to arrive in the Royal Duchy in 1958 were the heavy 117-ton A1A-A1A 2,000hp MAN-engined diesel-hydraulics. These were soon supplemented by a much more nimble B-B 78-ton version of the 'Warship' class, which produced 2,200hp from a pair of Maybach diesel engines (these later became Class 42; locos with MAN engines were Class 43s). With the new road bridge across the River Tamar looming above Brunel's railway bridge in the background, No D827 *Kelly* heads train 1C33, the down 'Cornishman', away from Saltash on 14 June 1961. *J. C. Beckett*

regularly be seen working long-haul freights. By the end of the 1960s the original five 'Warships' had been withdrawn and the future for all the diesel-hydraulic locomotives was bleak. The NBL Class 22s and the first of the Class 42s started to be withdrawn from 1968. From about 1970 the Class 46 variety of the 'Peak' class arrived in Cornwall and found a mixed-traffic role in the county for more than a decade. The last of the Class 22s was scrapped in 1972, and they were replaced by 1,250hp Class 25 Bo-Bos, which had been transferred from the LMR. By the end of the year the impressive Class 42/3 'Warships' had also been withdrawn, many having been in service for only ten years.

Due to the electrification of the line from Crewe to Glasgow the 2,750hp English Electric Class 50 Co-Co locomotives were displaced and decanted to the Western Region. By the end of 1973 the first example had arrived at Laira, and they were to be regular performers in Cornwall for more than 17 years. With the importation of the Class 50s, withdrawals of the last class of diesel-hydraulics, the Class 52s, continued apace; they were not compatible with modern rolling stock and by February 1977 they too had become extinct on BR metals.

In 1979 some of the reliable and well-established English Electric Class 37 Co-Cos started to replace the underpowered Class 25s. Eventually a small fleet would be present in Cornwall to handle the majority of china clay trains. With 1,750hp available (less at the rail) and weighing about 105 tons, the class were ideally suited to the task and their

Above: The ultimate in UK diesel-hydraulic locomotive design was the superb 2,700hp 'Western', later Class 52. A fleet of 74 locomotives operated in Cornwall from 1962 until 1977 and for some years they dominated the passenger train scene in the county. The two 12-cylinder Maybach engines produced an incredible sound and certainly No D1051 *Western Ambassador* could be heard some distance away as it climbed over Penadlake Viaduct, east of Bodmin Road station, with an up express in 1976. *Author*

Above: The 1,750hp English Electric Class 37s did not arrive in Cornwall until 1979 when they replaced less powerful and less reliable Class 25s. Their reign on local china clay duties lasted for just over 20 years until the already mentioned Class 66 locomotives were imported to the West Country. In original Railfreight livery No 37674 has 20 of the then new CDA hopper wagons in tow as it approaches Respryn Bridge, west of Bodmin Road (Parkway) station, in 1989. *Author*

This scene shows one of the newer freight flows in Cornwall. Sand, a bi-product of china clay processing, is being transported from Burngullow to Angerstein Wharf for eventual use in the building industry. Entrusted with one of the heavy 'as required' trains is Freightliner Heavy Haul No 66622 on 5 October 2007, seen leaving Coombe Viaduct at Saltash with the up loaded run. It is aesthetically pleasing to see the matching livery of both locomotive and wagons. *Author*

In years gone by trains full of holiday-makers in the summer months would work through to a number of Cornish destinations, many of them beside the seaside at the end of branch lines. After through train services to Falmouth ceased in 1979 Newquay became the only branch-line destination to receive long-distance through trains during the short summer season. It is fascinating to see 125mph main-line High Speed Train units running along a single line in Cornwall at 20mph. Crossing Goss Moor bridge with a Paddington-bound train on 8 September 2007 is a very clean First Great Western formation. *Author*

No book about transport heritage in Cornwall would be complete without reference to the Class 47 diesel locomotives from the Brush stable. Although not without their reliability problems, especially in the early days, these Sulzer-engined 2,580hp stalwarts have served the county in every capacity for more than 40 years. Seen just after arrival at Par station on 3 October 2007, the striking new Colas Rail livery carried by No 47749 *Demelza* is seen in Cornwall for the first time. With sister locomotive No 47727 *Rebecca* it would be put to work on Rail Head Treatment trains. *Author*

reign was to last for just over 20 years. In the same year the first of the squadron High Speed Train IC125 units came on stream and it was not long before the sleek units were working the prestigious 'Cornish Riviera' and 'Golden Hind' expresses. Deliveries continued and by May 1980 many of the Class 50s were transferred to other WR routes. Locomotive-hauled main-line trains became the exception, except for a few summer dated extras and the overnight sleeping car trains. In the meantime the Class 50s were being refurbished at Doncaster Works, giving them a 10-year life extension.

The Class 46s were next for the breaker's yard and in 1985 the few remaining Class 45 'Peaks' were banned west of Bristol, bringing to an end appearances in Cornwall, which had mainly been on Leeds or Newcastle trains and long distance freights. By the mid-1980s the various types of old diesel-mechanical units were beginning to feel their age and a new generation of multiple-units had begun to arrive in Cornwall. However, the new Class 142 'Skippers' lasted only about 18 months before being transferred away. Eventually all of the old units were replaced by Classes 150, 153 and 158. An interesting trial took place in Cornwall from August 1987 until February 1989 when a re-geared Class 50 locomotive was used on freight workings. Designated Class 50/1, No 50149 *Defiance* worked extensively on china clay trains.

Mention must be made of the humble Class 08 shunter. After a prolonged trial with some early types, such as the Class 03 and Class 10, the Class 08 became the standard motive power for yard and dock shunting and for use on minor lines such as the Wenford Bridge goods and the St Blazey to Ponts Mill run. They were also used in the docks at Carne Point, Fowey, and in the early days shared such duties with Blackstone-engined Class 10s. In recent times an ex-Southern Region Class 09 briefly appeared at St Blazey. There was also a resident shunting locomotive at Penzance, which amongst other things would work the empty sleeping car train to and from nearby Long Rock.

In February 1990 a brief trial was conducted in Cornwall using a Class 56 locomotive. The idea was for a single Class 56 to replace a pair of Class 37s on the long-distance air-braked freights. Nothing came of the experiment, but from about 1995 3,100hp Class 60s began to appear in Cornwall, performing the role envisaged for the Class 56. However, the development of greatest significance was the arrival at the beginning of 1999 of the first North American-built 126-ton 3,200hp high-tech Class 66 locomotive. These locomotives have revolutionised the UK motive power scene and in Cornwall they have halved the number of local china clay trains, simply because they can haul twice as much as their Class 37 predecessors. Class 66s now operate the overwhelming majority of freight trains in Cornwall.

Early in the present century some Class 47s were re-engined and updated to emerge with a General Motors prime mover and a Class 57 identifier. Class 57/6s are still being used on the overnight sleeper car trains. As regards passenger train workings, sleek but cramped 'Voyager' units now work cross-country services, with the faithful IC125 units still forming London trains. Class 67s regularly work excursion trains. Over the years many other diesel types have visited Cornwall and in total the number of different liveries appearing has been bewildering.

Fowey to the Camel

Cornwall's leading preserved railway is the Bodmin & Wenford Railway, an enlightened organisation that realises that history did not end in the 1960s. The railway caters for all

Through trains once worked from Bodmin Road (Bodmin Parkway since 1983) station on the River Fowey to Padstow on the River Camel. Part of this journey can now be made over the same trackbed as far as Boscarne Junction by preserved steam or diesel train, and on foot or by bicycle via the Camel Trail from there to Padstow. Pounding up the climb from the main line and away from the River Fowey on weed-covered track is Robert Stephenson & Hawthorn 0-6-0T No 7597 with a Bodmin General service in June 1997. *Author*

Contrary to the blinkered traction policy of many preserved lines, the Bodmin & Wenford Railway operates an interesting diesel locomotive fleet and even holds special diesel galas from time to time. One of the residents is 16-cylinder 2,700hp

Class 50 No 50042 *Triumph*, which regularly worked in Cornwall from 1975 until 1991. In the hugely attractive BR 'large logo' livery the immaculate locomotive gently pulls out of Bodmin Parkway station in September 1993. *Author*

types of railfan and is blessed with an excellent stable of steam locomotives, many of which originally worked in Cornwall, and a fine collection of diesels that also ran over Cornish metals. This finely balanced collection offers something for everybody with both steam galas and diesel days. The running lines comprise two distinct sections and slowly but surely a wonderful railway infrastructure is being created.

The two lines are from Bodmin General to Bodmin Parkway (formerly Bodmin Road) and also to Boscarne Junction, which is on an old 1834 alignment where lines once radiated to Bodmin North, Wenford Bridge and Wadebridge (and, from 1899, Padstow). Many years after closure of these railway lines most of the abandoned trackbed was converted to a long footpath and cycle path, which goes under the name of the Camel Trail, named after the River Camel that for some distance parallels the old railway lines. Together the Bodmin & Wenford Railway and the Camel Trail have produced a wonderful recreational facility of which both residents and visitors make good use.

The 1859 main line from Saltash to Penzance follows the infant River Fowey down the Glynn Valley and on to the ancient town of Lostwithiel. The Fowey is a short distance to the north of Bodmin Parkway station, but due to cost constraints and the local topography the main line could not be routed to the large and historically important town of Bodmin. The town was served by the Bodmin & Wadebridge Railway, but that provided a route to Wadebridge only, with no rail connections to the 'outside world'. In terms of enjoying a service to Plymouth, Exeter and London, Bodmin remained rail-less until the GWR opened its standard-gauge branch line into the town on 27 May 1887. There had been many earlier schemes to provide such a link, but for mainly financial reasons it had taken 28 years for Bodmin to join the GWR railway map.

The 3-mile 43-chain branch was not easy to build. The line had to climb some 300 feet and the permanent way included bridges, embankments, cuttings and curves, with some sections being graded at 1 in 37. At Bodmin General there was a fine granite terminus building, large goods shed, small engine shed and sidings. The 2-mile 56-chain connection to Boscarne Junction was opened on 3 September 1888 and it too was steeply graded, with similar 1 in 37 gradients. The L&SWR, which had purchased the old Bodmin & Wadebridge Railway (B&W), reached agreement with the GWR about joint running from Boscarne to Wadebridge.

The line from Wadebridge to Bodmin North and Wenford Bridge dates back to 1834 and has several claims to fame. It was the first standard-gauge line in Cornwall and the first to use steam locomotives. It was also the last line in the Duchy with steam-hauled trains. For decades the line was inextricably linked to the Beattie well tank locomotives. These veterans were built by Messrs Beyer Peacock of Gorton Works in Manchester in 1874/5 and arrived on the B&W in 1893. Except when under repair, three of the class worked at Wadebridge and on the Wenford line until 1962, a period of 69 years!

This workaday scene from June 1978 shows Bodmin General station long after it closed to passengers but well before the B&WR preservationists moved in. Class 08 350hp shunter No 08091 had just arrived from Wenford Bridge via Boscarne Junction and run round its train of eight china clay wagons and a brake-van. It is seen departing for Bodmin Road, where it will reverse for a third time on its way to St Blazey! On occasions the clay wagons were deposited in the sidings at Bodmin Road for collection. Sadly the wonderful old stone goods shed in the background was demolished shortly after this photograph was taken. *Author*

The Bodmin & Wenford Railway extended its sphere of operations from Bodmin General to Boscarne Junction in August 1996, providing a variety of routes and keeping options open for possible future extension towards Wadebridge. Long after the lines to Padstow, Wenford Bridge and Bodmin North closed the old trackbed was converted to a foot and cycle path known as the Camel Trail. This is a popular and well-used facility and at some locations evidence of its former use survives. This charming scene is at Hellandbridge on the old Wenford line in 2005 (SX065715). *Author*

The railways of Cornwall were not just about the Great Western Railway, and in some areas the London & South Western Railway (later Southern Railway) had a strong foothold. The Wadebridge to Wenford Bridge workings were operated by truly vintage Victorian locomotives from 1893 until 1962, a reign of 69 years! These were members of the '0298' class of 2-4-0 Beattie-designed well tanks. In this wonderful study at Wadebridge in the late 1920s a truly immaculate No 0298 poses with its crew and shunters. *Author's collection*

One cannot help but sense the enthusiasm and optimism of the bowler- and top-hatted local and railway dignities massed on the platform at Padstow to greet the first train in March 1899. Few would be able to contemplate the line closing in January 1967 after a life of only 67 years, especially as the closure was decided by the successors of the rival GWR! Today only Camel Trail cyclists and pedestrians arrive at Padstow, along the alignment of the old railway. *Brunel University*

A 1797 proposal to build a canal from Wadebridge to Dunmere never came to fruition, but in 1831 Sir William Molesworth of Pencarrow commissioned a survey to test the viability of building a railway from Wadebridge along the valley of the River Camel to Wenford Bridge, with branches to Ruthern Bridge and Bodmin. The survey was positive and a total cost of £26,000 was estimated. An Act was passed the following year and by August 1834 a locomotive and two wagons had worked to Ruthern Bridge. The grand opening of the 'main' line took place on 30 September 1834 when a gaily decorated train of 18 wagons and one other vehicle, fitted out for passengers, left Wadebridge with 300 on board, behind a locomotive called *Camel*.

Throughout the line's 149-year history there were never any passenger trains between Dunmere, near Boscarne Junction, and Wenford Bridge. They worked only from Padstow and Wadebridge to Bodmin North and, from 1888, Bodmin General. In the early years copper, iron, tin and lead ore were carried from Ruthern Bridge, Nanstallon and other loading points. There were numerous goods sidings along the Wenford line, which were used for fertiliser sand, road stone and, more importantly, china clay. Eventually a line was built beyond Wenford to De Lank Quarry via an inclined plane to convey granite (see the Quarries section). Traffic was booming and in the first year of operation 13,500 tons of sand and 2,320 passengers were carried. Mention must be made of a special train that ran from Wadebridge to Bodmin in 1840 where passengers witnessed the execution of the criminal Lightfoot brothers. By 1844 there had been a downturn and the Directors sold the line to the Cornwall & Devon Central Railway, soon itself taken over by the L&SWR, which was keen to keep the GWR out of North Cornwall.

In 1895 the L&SWR completed its North Cornwall line from Okehampton and Halwill Junction to Wadebridge and for the first time there was an alternative route into Cornwall other than the GWR main line. At the time Wadebridge was an important station with engine and goods sheds, sidings and a line onto the quay. The line was extended to Padstow, a distance of 5½ miles, in 1899. In 1906 halts were opened at Grogley, Nanstallon and Dunmere, but by 1923 the sand traffic had petered out, by then being dwarfed by china clay tonnages. In 1933 the lightly used Ruthern Bridge line closed, but otherwise little changed for decades and the railway continued to serve the local community, with trains hauled by a wide variety of motive power.

Post war passenger traffic peaked in the mid-1950s but, as mentioned in the Branch lines section, the 1960s brought about a close scrutiny of the profitability of branch and secondary lines. The reign of steam was coming to an end and all Southern lines in Cornwall had been taken over by the Western Region. In 1960 SR Class '02s' were replaced by '5700' class WR pannier tanks, and in 1962 the old Beattie Class '0298s' were replaced by outside-cylinder '1366' class pannier tanks. The '5700s' were in turn replaced by Ivatt 2-6-2Ts. Diesel multiple-units began to appear, as did Class 22 diesel locomotives. In 1964 economies were made when a small wooden exchange platform was built at Boscarne Junction, so that Bodmin General to Wadebridge service trains could set down passengers for Dunmere and Bodmin North, which was worked by a small four-wheeled railbus shuttling backwards and forwards up to five times per day (see p165). However, this operation and subsequent economies did not save the line. The remote and loss-making North Cornwall line closed in 1966, and from January 1967 all passenger services between Bodmin Road/General/North, Wadebridge and Padstow ceased. The Padstow line closed completely and the last goods train left Wadebridge in 1979. Finally, in 1983 the entire line from Wenford Bridge to Bodmin Road via Boscarne Junction and Bodmin General closed to all traffic. In the final years trains over this fascinating line were worked by Class 08 diesel shunters.

After the final passenger services had run, the Great Western Society leased the engine shed at Bodmin General, but this came to nothing and it was not until 1984 that the Bodmin Railway Preservation Society was formed. A successful share issue was placed and in 1987 the Cornish Steam Locomotive Preservation Society moved its stock from Bugle to Bodmin to join forces with the group. A Light Railway Order was approved in 1989 and in June 1990 regular services were run between Bodmin General and Bodmin Parkway. The second 'leg' of the by then Bodmin & Wenford Railway's network to Boscarne opened in August 1996. Since then the preservation society has not looked back; in fact, it is looking ahead to a possible extension to Wadebridge in the distant future.

Aircraft

One could be excused for thinking that, being located on the south-western tip of the UK mainland, aviation would not feature greatly in Cornwall's transport heritage. While this may be true in terms of the international scene, over the years there have been no fewer than 60 sites in Cornwall that have had some connection with flying. The first flight in Cornwall was almost 100 years ago when, in July 1910, Claude Grahame-White flew his fragile Farman biplane over Mount's Bay, near Penzance. His aircraft had arrived in Cornwall by train and was assembled in a field near Posandane. Before a fascinated public he took off and flew over the assembled British fleet, which had gathered for review by HM King George V, who never arrived due to bad weather.

It would be two years before the next flight, when Frenchman Henri Salmet flew his Bleriot monoplane to Bude, then on to many Cornish destinations, including Launceston, Bodmin, Newquay, Truro, Falmouth, Fowey and St Austell. On 12 November 1912 another milestone was reached when the first Cornishman qualified as a pilot; Lieutenant R. B. Kitson from Lanreath passed his test at Brooklands in Surrey. As a reminder of the perils of early aviation, Falmouth was to be one of nine resting stages for the 1913 Daily Mail Circuit of Britain seaplane race, but none of the entries got as far as Cornwall! In 1913 the first flight reached Land's End, and from 1914 exhibition flights followed thick and fast. During the First World War airships were

The history of flying and aeroplanes in Cornwall dates back to 1910 when Claude Grahame-White flew his frail Farman biplane across Mount's Bay, where the British fleet was anchored. The dismantled aeroplane had arrived by special railway carriage, which was unpacked at nearby Ponsandane. This started a long association between Cornwall and the aeroplane in respect of private, military and commercial flying activities. Probably the best-known passenger flights have been those between the Cornish mainland and the Isles of Scilly. British European Airways was formed on 1 August 1946 and operated De Havilland Dragon Rapide aircraft between Land's End Airport and St Mary's in the Isles of Scilly, where this picture was taken. Note the connecting bus. *Author's collection*

Opened in 1933, Newquay Airport has for some time been the most important in Cornwall in terms of long-distance flights. Over the years a large number of operators have flown from here, but many of the companies have either gone to the wall or been taken over. The total airport area included RAF St Mawgan, but since its recent decommissioning the County Council has had to assume runway maintenance, air traffic control and fire-fighting responsibilities. In this 2007 scene an Air Southwest flight has just landed; the company flies from Newquay to London Gatwick, Bristol, Dublin, Leeds Bradford, Manchester and Cardiff. *Author*

based in Cornwall, their primary activity being submarine patrols. A base was established at Royal Naval Air Station Mullion in June 1916 and was known as Lizard Airship Station. Other bases were established such as the two-airship station at Bude.

The First World War also saw a number of early military aircraft based in Cornwall. Again Mullion featured as an airbase with others at Newlyn and Padstow, as well as RNAS Tresco on Scilly. A variety of both seaplanes, or more correctly floatplanes, and landplanes were used. The Royal Air Force was established on 1 April 1918, but shortly afterwards the war ended and most of the bases were quickly decommissioned. During the 1920s and 1930s commercial aviation began to establish itself in Cornwall and small airfields appeared, most of the 'airports' being designated farmers' fields. By 1924 some aviators were providing 4-minute pleasure flights for the general public at 5 shillings a go, and flying circuses and display teams were performing in Cornwall. The first land aircraft to visit the Isles of Scilly was in August 1929.

The first scheduled passenger service in Cornwall was run by Provincial Airways Ltd, which offered two flights per day between Plymouth and Hayle from April 1934, later extended to Newquay and Penzance before the company went into liquidation in 1935. In 1937 Channel Air Ferries started a service from St Just, which became Land's End Airport, to the Isles of Scilly. The aircraft was a DeHavilland Dragon flown by a New Zealander, Captain D. L. Dustin. The flight duration was 20 minutes, there were four passengers and the fare was £1. Dustin was killed on a June evening in 1938 when the Dragon crash-landed at Land's End. The six passengers were injured but survived. In May 1938 the same company started a Plymouth to Land's End service. By the end of the 1930s further Cornish airports were established, and in May 1939 Western Airways started a Swansea to Penzance service, which also called at Newquay.

By the end of the 1930s the Second World War was looming and surveys were conducted in Cornwall to find potential new airfield sites, which included RAF Cleave near Bude, RAF St Eval near Newquay, RAF St Merryn, RAF Perranporth, RAF

Left: A Royal Navy Jetstream T Mark 2 aircraft flies over St Michael's Mount in Mount's Bay, the scene of the first ever flight in Cornwall in 1910. This type of aircraft was still flying out of RNAS Culdrose in Cornwall with 750 Squadron at the end of 2008. During the Second World War Cornwall was covered in military airfields and each had a specific role with dedicated squadrons. The US Air Force also made a significant contribution in the lead-up to VE Day. In addition to fixed-wing aircraft, helicopters have had a significant presence during recent decades, especially in the Search and Rescue role based at RNAS Culdrose. *RNAS Culdrose, courtesy of J. Hicks*

Back in 1963 BEA was looking for a replacement for its ageing DH Rapides, and procured two Sikorsky S-61N helicopters that could carry three times the number of passengers as a fixed-wing Rapide and were better able to deal with operating restrictions at St Mary's. Initially Land's End Airport was used, but a new 14-acre heliport facility was planned for Penzance, where the weather was better and where there were satisfactory rail and road connections. As seen in March 2007 the Sikorsky helicopters are still in action and G-BCEB *The Isles of Scilly* departs from Penzance with a morning flight. BA sold its helicopter subsidiary in 1985, the new company being renamed British International Helicopters. *Author*

Land's End Airport with its grass runways was opened in September 1937 when four passengers flew to the Isles of Scilly in a De Havilland Dragon. The airport still retains a 'yesteryear' atmosphere, possibly due to the seemingly slow pace of life and the white lettering on the old corrugated roof below the control tower. In the foreground is Isles of Scilly Skybus, Britten-Norman Islander aircraft G-SBUS. The Islander has been in production for more than 40 years and its sales record is impressive. Beyond is a single-engined Cessna 172 'Scenic Flights' aircraft of Westward Airways. There is also a flying school at the airport. *Author*

Portreath, RAF Predannack near Mullion, RAF Trebelzue, and RAF Davidstow. These airfields had multiple roles and boasted a remarkable array of both British and American aircraft types, from many different squadrons. RAF Trebelzue was renamed RAF St Mawgan on 24 February 1943. Flying-boats were based at Falmouth. All of the Cornish airfields were bombed by the German Luftwaffe on a regular basis and the successes and failures, the bravery and sacrifices, make fascinating reading. Overall Cornwall played a vital role during the Second World War.

From 1946 civil flying became derestricted and small independent airlines began to appear. British European Airways was formed in 1946 and began to operate DH Dragon Rapides on the Scillies route. Charter firm Island Air Services was also founded. Over the next 60 years there would appear a plethora of domestic air services from within the UK and the Channel Islands to Cornwall. Many of the routes were short-lived and a large number of minor airlines were established, taken over, amalgamated and closed down. The main focus was on Newquay Airport, which was for many years effectively part of RAF St Mawgan.

Among the airlines that have operated into Cornwall since the 1940s are Aquila Airways, Fingland Aviation, Murray Chown Aviation, Melba Airways, Olley Air Services, Starways, Mayflower Air Services, Scillonian Air Services, British Westpoint, Westpoint Aviation, British Eagle International Airlines, Solair Flying Services, BEA, British International Airways, British Midland, Scillonia Airways, Dan-Air, Westward Airways, Brymon Airways, Severn Airways, Air Anglia, Skybus, British Airways, Air SouthWest, Flybe, Ryanair, BMIbaby, Isles of Scilly Skybus and many others.

All indications are that Newquay Airport is growing, with routes to London, Exeter, Bristol, Dublin, Leeds, Manchester and Cardiff, and although airlines and routes continue to change, there is a core business that will ensure its future. A record total of

400,000 passengers used the airport in 2007. However, the busiest route has been by helicopter from Penzance and by fixed-wing aircraft from Land's End and Newquay Airports to the Scilly Isles, with well over a quarter of a million passengers carried per annum. The military continue to make use of Cornwall, for example from RNAS Culdrose, but St Mawgan has recently been decommissioned.

Above: Cornish airfields made a very significant contribution to the Second World War effort. Hundreds of British, American, Polish and Australian airmen gave their lives in defence of these lands. The rapidly constructed Cornish airbases were regularly attacked by the Luftwaffe but fortunately the list of successful sorties and engagements is longer than the many disasters that befell our brave airmen. One of the most evocative sights in Cornwall is the remains of the wild and desolate Davidstow airfield at SX 150850, the highest in the UK at an elevation of 970ft. As one views the crumbling concrete runways, the shell of the old concrete control tower and the grazing sheep, seen here in May 2008, it is now difficult to imagine the frenetic activity that took place during the 1942 to 1945 period. After decommissioning, the site was briefly used as a car racing circuit but appalling weather conditions and a remote location resulted in abandonment in the early 1950s. *Author*

Left: Perranporth Airport was another former RAF airfield. It was opened in April 1941 and was operational until the end of the war. During the Second World War the clifftop establishment was host to a variety of squadrons and aircraft types and its operational logs make fascinating reading. It was best known for its Spitfires and original pens survive. There is also a touching memorial to those who served. Most bases were abandoned but Perranporth became a viable civil airport and the only one in Cornwall with tarmac runways. There is a private flying club, a gliding and parachute centre and a cafe on site. This 2007 view shows the airport's firefighting capability comprising a splendid vintage Land Rover! *Author*

Main Location Index